Exploring Movie Construction and Production

Exploring Movie Construction and Production

What's so exciting about movies?

John Reich

Open SUNY Textbooks

© 2017 John Reich

ISBN: 978-1-942341-47-5 print

This publication was made possible by a SUNY Innovative Instruction Technology Grant (IITG). IITG is a competitive grants program open to SUNY faculty and support staff across all disciplines. IITG encourages development of innovations that meet the Power of SUNY's transformative vision.

Published by Open SUNY Textbooks

Milne Library
State University of New York at Geneseo
Geneseo, NY 14454

This book was produced using Pressbooks.com, and PDF rendering was done by PrinceXML.

Dedication

For my wife, Suzie, for a lifetime of beautiful memories, each one a movie in itself.

Contents

Acknowledgments   ix
Introduction   1

Part I: Construction

1. What Is the Theme? Why Do We Need It?   7
2. What Is Genre and How Is It Determined?   16
3. What Are the Mechanics of Story and Plot?   33
4. How Are the Characters Portrayed?   39

Part II: Production

Prologue   49
5. What Is Directing?   50
6. What Is Cinematography?   54
7. What Is Editing?   62
8. What Is Sound?   67

Conclusion: What's So Exciting about Movies? – Novice Answers   72
Production Assignment   75
Cinematography Assignment   77
Future Viewing   81
Bibliography   83
Photo Attributions   85

Acknowledgments

With love and thanks to: Bethany, Rachael, Tim, Nick, Timmy, Dominic, and Zachary.

Special thanks to two excellent and helpful book reviewers for putting me on the right track.

Thanks to Dominic C. and the other students at Genesee Community College for their contribution.

Thanks to Heather and Alec.

Introduction

Why do we get excited when we think about going to the movies?

Do you love a movie but when asked why, you can't explain it?

What is it about watching movies that makes it one of our favorite pastimes? Is it the star of the movie? Is it the hype about the movie? Is it because it is an action movie or thriller? Do you like comedies so you can laugh? Most people do.

Genesee Community College students made the following comments about the joy of watching comedy movies.

> "(I like) being able to watch a movie and relieving any sadness and negativity (in me) by laughing and realizing things are not so bad."

> "I enjoy a movie because it takes me away from my problems in my life for a short period of time."

> "I can escape life a little bit. I can just laugh and not think about work or school or any other stresses in life."

> "I like to watch (a) comedy on a sad day because I can smile and laugh about it later."

> "I like comedy movies because I love to laugh. Most comedies deal with real life things, which make me enjoy watching them."

Movies offer much more. Do you like suspense in a movie?

How much of a movie do you remember two weeks after seeing it? Have you ever wanted to keep your adrenalin up after watching a suspenseful movie or keep your euphoric mood up after watching a comedy?

This book will assist you in answering the above questions and in giving you a new perspective on watching movies. After reading it, the students who made the above comments have a new, more fulfilling appreciation for movies now. This book will instruct you in cinematic terminology to help you better comprehend the construction and production of movies, giving you a better understanding why you like them.

If you have not watched a lot of movies, this book will give you a solid foundation for better understanding the movies you watch. It is different from other textbooks because it is more of an aid to anyone who does not have a good background in the construction and production of movies.

The areas covered in this book are theme, genre, narrative structure, character and character development, story, directing, cinematography, editing and sound. These areas are covered in this specific order so you can see the formation of a movie from the theme, or purpose, through to its completion.

The definitions of the key words in film are given simply and in a straightforward manner. The definitions have been put into a formula so they are in the simplest form for easy recall or remembering.

This book is designed in this manner because, as a college film instructor at a community college for 18 years, I found that the biggest difficulty students have with a film course is the textbook. Other textbooks give examples from numerous movies to demonstrate a particular term. Most of the movies used in other textbooks, the students have not seen, resulting in the students not comprehending the technical film terms and rendering the textbook useless.

A book on film should be about film terminology and the understanding of it. Movies then become more appreciated when watched, resulting in better understanding of the movie and the terminology.

After teaching film for so many years, I still feel like a novice at times. This is why a good textbook that explains the primary points of movie framework, construction, and production is essential for beginning students to benefit from a movie course.

This statement was verified by Dominic, a former student of mine at Genesee Community College, who took Popular Cinema and Thriller Films between 2013 and 2014.

> Having taken a couple of film courses, I can say that the current way textbooks for film courses are laid out is flawed. They really don't provide any significant benefit to the student, because you don't really use them in the course, and a majority of the learning is done through discussing terms, genres, and other film-related things in class. This is true for multiple courses, because the textbooks simply don't provide you with what you need to succeed in the course. The textbooks discuss terms and define types of genres and subgenres by using specific movies. The problem with this is that you may not have seen the movie that is being used to discuss the genres and subgenres and terms, so you may not get a complete understanding of the subject being discussed. In previous textbooks I have used, I have only seen one movie that was being discussed in the textbook.[1]

Exploring Movie Construction & Production: What's So Exciting About Movies from a Novice Point of View?! explains and demonstrates film terminology by using three movies, which are watched by the students at the beginning of the semester, and before reading this book, and trying to comprehend the extended hypothetical examples.

So, as you read this book, rest assured that you do not need an extensive movie background. Everyone starts at the same point, and they progress together. You can logically and easily understand the terminology and the extended hypothetical examples from watching the three freely accessible movies listed below.

The following movie background information is courtesy of the Internet Movie Database (IMDb) and the American Film Institute.

The first movie is *The Front Page*, released in 1931, starring Adolphe Menjou and Pat O'Brien, and directed by Lewis Milestone. The Caddo Company, Inc. was the production company, and the movie was distributed by United Artists Corporation. This movie is presented on YouTube by the Described and Captioned Media Program. This version is captioned because of the age of the movie.

https://www.youtube.com/watch?v=cS49lyn7568

The second movie is *Detour*, released in 1945, starring Tom Neal, Ann Savage, and Claudia Drake, and directed by Edgar G. Ulmer. PRC Pictures, Inc. was the production company, and the movie was distributed by Producing Releasing Corporation (Pathe Industries, Inc.).

https://youtu.be/tap67KjjPu8

The third movie is *Cyrano de Bergerac*, released in 1950, starring Jose Ferrer, Mala Powers, and William Prince, and directed by Michael Gordon. Stanley Kramer Productions, Inc. was the production company, and the movie was distributed by United Artists Corporation. This movie is presented on YouTube by Charles Ewing Smith.

https://www.youtube.com/watch?v=K_r0Vcf4IVQ

After watching the movies, extended hypothetical examples that contain fictitious characters and situations are used to demonstrate a specific term or detail. The extended hypothetical examples can be altered, as needed, and used as assignments. No matter whether an assignment is given or not, the extended hypothetical examples can be used, discussed, and modified in the classroom by you and/or the instructor to demonstrate and help you better understand a particular aspect of the film.

We will initiate the explanations of the extended hypothetical examples in their simplest form: a boy and a girl, named Jack and Suzie, respectively. They are nondescript at this time, so their personalities and actions can be adjusted as we discuss the different terms, concepts, and ideas in each of the chapters presented in this book.

All other background, story, atmosphere, and technology will be added as we go along. Let's see what adventures we can throw them into as we talk about the construction and production of a movie.

Regarding this format, Dominic continued by commenting that:

> This is why using hypothetical examples would be more useful. Creating hypothetical examples can cover a genre, sub-genre, or term better than specific movies can. Using a specific movie to define the, let's say, action genre, wouldn't be as helpful as a hypothetical situation. As mentioned, what if you haven't seen that specific movie? Will you completely understand this genre if you haven't seen the example being discussed? Also a specific movie may not cover all parts of a term or genre, like a hypothetical situation can. To elaborate, someone who hasn't seen a lot of action movies is provided with a specific action movie, as an example in their film class, and now every action movie they see, after this class, will be compared to this one action movie, because that's what they were taught an action movie is. A hypothetical situation would be able to give you a more broad sense of action movies as opposed to comparing all action movies to one action movie. These hypothetical examples will allow you to think creatively when discussing genres, subgenres, movie terms, and also allow you to understand the content better as well as actually making the textbook for film class relevant and useful again.[2]

With watching these three movies and building the extended hypothetical examples, you are not restricted. You are only limited by your imagination in understanding the terms and creating the concepts initiated by those terms.

At the end of each chapter in the textbook, additional movies will be suggested for viewing. These movies are good examples of further exemplifying the topic discussed in the chapter. The students will have other actual movies besides *The Front Page*, *Detour*, and *Cyrano de Bergerac* to demonstrate the extended hypothetical examples and to help assist them in understanding the terminology.

So let us begin to understand, analyze, envision, and create a deeper appreciation of movies.

1 Dominic C., in discussion with the author, May 2014.

2 Dominic C., in discussion with the author, May 2014.

Part I: Construction

1. What Is the Theme? Why Do We Need It?

Webster's Encyclopedic Unbridged Dictionary of the English Language defines theme as "a subject of discourse, discussion, meditation, or composition; topic: . . . ."[3] In other words, a theme is the idea, premise, or purpose of a movie. It is the whole reason why movies are made.

The theme is the heart of the movie. The movie is regulated by the theme. The theme is why people go to the movies. It is not because of the characters, story, plot, cinematography, or genre. All of these elements are regulated by the theme. They demonstrate how the theme is displayed, yet most people do not know or understand what the theme is when they go to see a movie and when they discuss the movie afterward.

The producer, who does the hiring and firing of employees and finds the money to make the movie, picks the theme. Once the producer picks the theme for a movie, he or she will hire a writer, to create the theme, and a director, to express the theme on film. Or, the producer can look through completed scripts to find a script that exemplifies his or her preferred theme.

By the end of the construction of the theme, the script will contain a story or action plus a plot. Both of these elements, combined, produce the character development, which yields or reflects the theme. Essentially, all aspects of the movie revert back to the theme.

A short definition for the theme is: **S**tory (**A**ction) + **P**lot = **C**haracter **D**evelopment **Y**ielding the **T**heme.

The above elements of the story, plot, and character development give meaning to the theme. These elements, as well as being discussed with regard to the theme, will be discussed from different viewpoints in succeeding chapters.

The theme—or idea or premise—of a movie can be expressed in one sentence. It may seem unusual that the purpose of a multi-million-dollar movie project begins with one sentence, and it may seem unusual that, at the end of the project with the completed movie, it all boils down to one sentence, but it really does.

Examples of themes can be analyzed by the period or decade in which a movie was made. Themes, and the resulting movies, are often a product and reflection of the social, economic or political climate of that time in history.

The importance of the theme cannot be overemphasized. The whole purpose and perspective of a movie is transformed when the theme changes.

Beginning with the early part of the 20th century, we will go through the different decades of the century into the 21st century, and we will briefly discuss the history of American society, in general, and how themes and, ultimately, movies changed during the century. This discussion will enable you to better understand how the actual construction of a movie changes in order to gain acceptance by the public.

Movie acceptance is based on themes. The themes indicated throughout this chapter change and develop. Seeing this change and development will help students understand themes and why movies are the way they are in the modern age.

Let's take a quick run through the decades with Jack and Suzie to see how they and their stories changed as history and society changed. We can speculate about how the producer determined the best way to demonstrate themes through the decades.

The 1920s

The 1920s, before the Great Depression, was a period of great prosperity, where society changed quicker than people could keep up. However, it was also a period of rigid class structure, the fear of Communism, and attempts to limit the power of the unions. The period also gave society Prohibition, flappers, parties, and gangsters.

What type of theme would emerge from this decade? Even though there is a certain segment of society who wants to see the real society of the period, people usually do not want to be reminded of the ills of society, and they want to escape them. But, the question is, "How large a segment of the population wants to go to see escapist fare, to forget the reality of the world for a few brief hours? The producer may attempt this type of theme in the belief that it would attract more people.

Like many times throughout history, producers have to take a risk on the possible movie-going taste of the public at that time in history, and they hope that the movie theme will make money. The producer may want to take a chance on a theme about the ills of a rigid class structure that does not allow true happiness—even though that is what people are trying to escape.

The premise for the theme could be shown by having Jack as a rich entrepreneur who falls in love with Suzie, a poor girl from the slums of New York City. However, he cannot have a lasting relationship with her because the rigid class structure of society at that time would not allow it. Because of society, they both become lost, defeated souls by the end of the movie.

How would Jack and Suzie present a theme that would allow an escape from the harsh realities of society? Jack could be a swashbuckler from the sixteenth 16th century or an adventurer in the Middle East in a period long before the 1920s, or he could even be a handsome cowboy. These three character types are complete escapist fare.

In the 1920s, what type of character would Suzie play to Jack's dashing hero? A damsel in distress would be the perfect character. She could be the damsel who is kidnapped, and Jack runs to her rescue, fighting untold odds to obtain her release. The action would be far beyond any type of reality, but the audiences would not care because they would be highly entertained, and they would be escaping the reality of their society for a little while at the movie theatre.

The 1920s was a period where the above characters could exist because of the rigid gender structure.

The 1930s

In the 1930s, during the Great Depression, people went to the movies to escape the harsh realities of poverty. Movies were one of the few, and possibly the only business, that showed a profit during the Depression, because people had such a strong desire to escape their lives for a while. So the theme in the 1930s could be emotional optimism—no matter how unrealistic it was.

Jack might be an unemployed artist, and Suzie a rich socialite who sees his paintings and likes them. After many humorous mishaps caused by Suzie, a relationship develops and builds until they finally live happily ever after.

The producer could have attempted this theme, even though it might be thin and unbelievable, to give people hope and the courage to return to reality. And with hope as the theme, the producer believes he could make money from the movie.

However, before the strict enforcement of the moral guidelines of the Motion Picture Production Code, the Hays Code, in 1934, and the harsh realities of the Great Depression, how people actually lived and acted could have been shown. The producer, in this situation, could become a great reformer.

Jack could be a World War I war hero, who has a good job and a girlfriend, Suzie. The Great Depression strikes. Jack loses his job, having to leave town to find work in another locality. However, he doesn't have the money for a vehicle. So, he walks from town to town, looking for work. Suzie gets word from a stranger that Jack has been hurt because he had to take a dangerous job to make enough money to marry Suzie. Suzie gets together enough money to go and see Jack, but she is too late. Jack died. This would really strike an emotional chord of the audiences of the 1930s. The audience might believe that these people are worse off than they were.

What would be the theme for this movie? Could the theme be one of encouragement to the people of this decade? Could the theme of the story be that no matter what happens, you have to try to continue—even if, at the end, you die?

In July 1934, when the Hays Code began to be strictly enforced by Joseph Breen, would the theme change? What would it change to? The story would be greatly toned down. Jack and Suzie would be boyfriend and girlfriend. Jack would lose his job because of the Depression, but he would become successful for another company. Jack and Suzie would obtain happiness by the end of the movie.

Let's move to the 1940s to see what themes that decade had to offer. I hope you are seeing how the theme of a movie is developed.

The 1940s

In the 1940s, World War II interrupted the lives of people around the world. Families were torn apart with men fighting in the South Pacific, Africa, or Europe. The families remaining at home in the United States wondered what would happen to their loved ones and themselves if the Axis powers won the war. With families ripped apart, society, the economy, and the labor force had to make adjustments to continue to function during those difficult times.

The producer had a wealth of choices to choose from and many locales around the world to consider. From all this material the producer would wonder what type of film would entice people to go to the movie theatres. The theme could possibly state that whatever needs to be done is done in order to bring the families together again or in hope of bringing families together again.

This theme could be demonstrated by Suzie going to work in a factory but keeping that special time of day when she writes her daily letter to her husband, Jack, who is in the infantry in Europe. This theme could be one of eternal love and never letting it die. This would be the type of theme that displayed the emotion that much of the American public was feeling, at the time, so this could be very popular.

Another theme that would have been popular during this period is one of action and winning the war in Europe and Japan. This type of movie would show Jack as an action soldier doing whatever it takes to obtain victory. Suzie would not be in this movie at all. It would be a "guy" movie with masculine themes.

The third theme could be dark and gloomy because the future was unclear, so everybody had to carve out his or her own existence in order to exist in the new world without families and the security of loved ones being close at hand. This theme could be demonstrated by Jack and Suzie working against one another to obtain something. Jack would be a loner thinking he is helping Suzie, while all the time she is working against him. Jack would not know this.

The movie with a theme of "do not trust anyone" might have been successful as a wake-up call to people at that time that hope and a happy ending were not always possible. This is a realistic theme that a producer might believe the public needed to understand. Once again, some people like this type of movie, so the producer could have believed this themed movie would be successful.

As society gets more complicated, movie themes become more numerous, and the earlier themes would have to be adjusted. As we move on, how would themes evolve? Would they become more numerous? How did or does society change?

The 1950s

The 1950s was a decade of huge change in the United States. In *United States v. Paramount Pictures*,[4] a Hollywood antitrust case from 1948 broke up the Studio System, so movies became more competitive. This was also the period of McCarthyism, the Second Red Scare, and the Hollywood Blacklist, along with the Korean Conflict and the beginning of the Cold War.

At the same time, suburbia began, as everyone after World War II wanted to have their own homes. Within suburbia, the family unit was very strong. The popularity of drive-in movies and television provided activities that the whole family could be involved in, in order to keep the family unit strong.

People wanted more in their movies than in past decades. As competition for audiences grew, the themes had to become more sophisticated than before. The themes became more realistic with characters that had more depth and situations that were more adult. These realistic themes brought characters that had faults like the next door neighbor or somebody who the audience knew at work. The acting style changed, portraying the characters more three dimensionally and realistically. Themes from previous decades were no longer valid.

What type of theme would be reflective of the American society of the 1950s? What would be next for Jack and Suzie? How about a theme that simply states what is best for the family? If you were Jack or Suzie, what would you want that would encompass all the aforementioned occurrences of the 1950s?

Perhaps Suzie would want to get married and have a family, since this was an important part of the 1950s. Suzie, though, would have more individuality doing this than women during the decades of the 1930s or 1940s.

Jack, as the male head of the household, would be instrumental in providing the theme. The theme would be "doing the right thing" because it is what was best for the family. How could this theme be exemplified? What type of person would Jack be?

Jack would be any man who lived in a large city, small town, or a new suburban location. He could have had a job working in a factory or a position with a corporation. The job would be nothing glamorous, but he would be responsible to his family and his employer. Jack would be involved in something or he would have witnessed something where he had to decide what action to take for the betterment of Suzie, their relationship, and maintaining their family unit.

Suzie would have supported him in any action he took. Jack would do what he believed to be the most truthful scenario to arrive at the best course of action. To Jack, he performed the correct action, even though nothing would be any longer the same, but the family unit and his relationship with Suzie would have survived the best way possible. This means family above the job, if necessary. Generally, family and job survive if everything is done the ethical way.

The 1950s flourished with themes such as this one, and people continued to go to the movies.

The 1960s

The first half of the 1960s looked very much like the end of the 1950s. The theme, reflecting on Suzie or Jack as a tarnished person, could occur but within the acceptance of the morals of society. In addition, Jack would still be the dominate influence.

The theme, for instance, could be a social change that Suzie makes but Jack would orchestrate the change for his benefit. If Jack made the social change, then he ultimately succeeds on his own. Suzie could assist, but she would only be a supporting character.

However, a big difference in the liberality of the American society, or at least part of American society, occurred between the mid- and late 1960s. In the mid-1960s, society began a massive change in issues about fighting overseas and social norms, so a big change in movie themes should also be noticeable. This change was brought about by many factors. McCarthyism and the government, in general, became the enemy, along with corporate management. Animosity toward the Vietnam Conflict grew along with protesting the actions of the American government.

The role of women in movies was changing, caused by the second-wave feminism from the early 1960s. Women were becoming a controlling influence in the movies that were produced. Women were no longer defenseless and in need of male support. If you were part of the American public that experienced the change in the late 1960s, specifically from 1965 to the end of the decade, you wanted to watch and see the changed American public on the big screen.

In this type of changing thematic climate, we would begin discussing Suzie as the main character. She could be hard working and attempting to reach some degree of success. However, with this type of theme, Suzie would have a turning point where she discovers other people finding ways to circumvent getting ahead in a company or government by manipulating people to get the promotion rather than by working hard. In this type of atmosphere, Suzie would ultimately be found out by Jack. Jack would make sure, by the climax of the movie, that Suzie would receive her just rewards for the actions she took.

The 1970s

Let's jump to the 1970s, which was a decade of great social change that initially began being engineered in the second half of the 1960s. In this decade, the producer might have wanted a theme of accomplishment, especially for Suzie, because this was a period of enforcing gender equality. Title IX of the Education Amendments Act passed in 1972, providing educational equality for males and females.

"Never give up" may be Suzie's motto as she works hard at cutting through prejudice and bureaucracy to accomplish her goal. What type of theme would exhibit educational equality at the beginning?

The theme could be growth and development to gain what you want because prejudice has stopped you in the past. Or, sometimes you had to get angry to get what you wanted.

Suzie could express the desire to achieve educational equality by portraying a college student. She could start off by being naïve when she first begins her college career. She is the college student that just goes because it is free for her, and people believed in the 1970s that high school graduates should go to college because it was part of growing up. So, Suzie would start college and begin to wander aimlessly through the first semester of courses with no specific purpose or outcome in mind.

Then Suzie meets someone, Jack. Jack would have a need to succeed because he has a sibling to support because his parents have died. Jack is older and has realized he has to make something of himself in order to survive.

Suzie likes Jack and looks up to him. She even wants to mirror his desire for success. However, Suzie runs into a prejudicial roadblock at college. She fights to succeed and Jack assists her in her quest.

The theme would be very well expressed and quite pertinent in the 1970s, the decade of innovative themes, as women started to come into their own.

The 1980s

We have now progressed to the theme period of the 1980s. The notion of "searching" is often a central theme throughout history, but it seemed even more relevant in our rapidly changing society. What types of themes were predominant in the 1980s?

This decade contained the computer age, but also assassinations and act-alone crimes occurred. Was this the beginning of the age of negativity? Women became more prominent in space, movies, and politics. More women started to direct movies, but AIDS began in the 1980s too.

With these thoughts in your mind, what one or two themes would be the most reflective and expressive of the 1980s?

Jack believes that the 1980s is his decade. Jack wants to become all that he can be even though he has started a relationship with a girl, Suzie, he met in college. He tells Suzie that he is going to make his mark in the world, making a million dollars or two while he is at it. He adds that she can come along for the ride if she wants to.

She is just something added to his list, but Suzie decides to go with Jack's desired rise in power. Jack is slowly becoming successful, but through a mistake, while getting a physical to take an overseas trip, he contracts AIDS.

Suzie stays with Jack through the bad times with AIDS. She nurses him as best as she can. This was the beginning of an age where Suzie had the opportunity to follow her dreams. Nonetheless, she decides to keep a low profile and stay with Jack. Toward the end, Jack realizes what Suzie has sacrificed and done for him. He realizes what a jerk he has been for years and that the love of a person is more important than all the monetary rewards and accolades that one can achieve.

The theme is quite clear here.

The 1990s

The 1990s signified a new beginning. The old order of control and prejudice that had lasted for decades began to vanish. The Soviet Union was dissolved. Apartheid laws were repealed. The Cold War ended. And, wars, like Operation Desert Storm, occurred along with riots in Los Angeles, the bombing of the World Trade Center in 1995, and the Rwandan Genocide. And, the internet grew exponentially.

The 1990s was a foreshadowing of the 21st century violence and harsher conditions. What type of themes could be given to this decade? What type of people would Jack and Suzie be in this decade?

The theme that would predominate would be isolation in order to try to keep all of the negative changes away from Jack and Suzie. Being the 1990s Suzie would be doing the protecting this time.

Suzie is a single mother raising her son, Jack, as best she can. One day, she takes Jack from their home in the suburbs in the United States and moves to an out-of-the-way island. They establish a home. Conditions are harsh, and the lifestyle is not the same as their hometown. They adapt, but the progress and gratification that they were used to is missing. They return to their original home, knowing they have to adapt to a changing society rather than running away from it.

Based on the above, what other theme is appropriate? No matter what the circumstance, people are resilient. No matter how bad the conditions, people have to have hope.

Certain curious individuals exist who will stop a negative future by researching, discovering, and trying to make the necessary changes so the potential future does not occur. In this example, Jack and Suzie are economic researchers exploring ideas and potential trends to identify latent disasters that could occur. They discover a potential shortage of oil, which is beginning to get bad in the 1990s and will only become worse in the 21st century. They try to convince people of the disastrous situations that will happen but no one wants to listen.

Knowing what the future brings, how would you continue this story? What would the ending be?

The 21st Century

The 1980s and the 1990s have blossomed to a crescendo of computer advances, hatred, and violence. The ultimate culmination of the hatred and violence occurred on September 11, 2001 with terrorists attacking the Pentagon in Washington, DC and destroying the World Trade Center Twin Towers in New York City.

However, the progress that began in the 1980s with computers and electronics continued. This is a Brave New World where anything is possible. What theme can best express this era? How about trying to understand the actions of a few?

Jack and Suzie are a married, middle-aged couple living in a small town near a big city. They live alone because their children are married and have moved away out of necessity to find good jobs. They try to understand why all this violence occurs, but they cannot. So they decide to retire early and travel around the United States to find answers to their thoughts of why certain people act in a violent manner. Their conclusion becomes the same and is reflective of a 1990s theme. The ultimate conclusion is acceptance.

The notion of "searching" is often a central theme throughout history, but it seems even more relevant in our rapidly changing society. Themes also review the other side of the situation where, instead of searching, people dive into the current social ideals to see what they can get.

How could this theme be demonstrated? Let's follow an example of this theme.

Jack and Suzie are married and decide to join their friends in a competition to see how much money they can make. They are in it for "me" or themselves. They have been ego-centric for years as their friends disappear from their view. They ostracize themselves from their friends in an effort to bilk the public and make as much money as they can.

Finally, they realize, once they have made a fortune that they do not know what they really have? What have they really made? Are they fulfilled, or are their lives emptier than before they began? They find that they are all alone because nobody in their circles has reached their level of wealth.

Chapter Conclusion

You can see that history and society explain why certain themes became prevalent. The themes presented in this chapter are only examples of the types of themes that movies could be based upon that reflect a particular time period or decade.

Themes changed in subsequent decades as producers made movies they believed people would go to see. A theme is only limited by a director's or writer's imagination. A producer may believe that escapists or nostalgic fare may be popular and successful in a particular decade rather than exemplifying the ills of the society of that decade. If these movies are successful, they demonstrate the desires and interests of the current society. People want to see these types of movies because of the conditions their lives are in and the society that they live in. Whenever a theme is made into a movie, the producer is always taking a chance at what will be a popular, money-making success.

The remaining chapters in this book are more movie specific, discussing aspects of movies, themselves, rather than why we watch certain movies. We will discuss different formats that will make these previously described themes successful. The reason behind making movies is multi-faceted. You, as the producer, want people to think and analyze an idea, while packaging it so the viewer thinks it is just a piece of entertainment.

Before you advance into the next chapter, though, what would you say the themes of *The Front Page*, *Detour*, and *Cyrano de Bergerac* are? What are the main ingredients that go into creating these themes?

Now we will discuss why we get excited to go to the movies!

Let's begin by looking at the general raw ingredients that go into a particular type of movie to form a specific genre. What are also the main ingredients that go into creating the specific genres of *The Front Page*, *Detour*, and *Cyrano de Bergerac*?

Further Viewing

With the completion of this chapter, movies to watch that that are excellent examples of themes that have been produced throughout the different decades are:

- *Broken Blossoms*, 1919, directed by D. W. Griffith, starring Lillian Gish, Richard Barthelmess, and Donald Crisp. This was a popular movie of the period. Does the theme reflect the decade?
- *My Man Godfrey*, 1936, directed by Gregory La Cava, starring William Powell and Carole Lombard. How reflective of the decade is the theme in this movie?
- *The Maltese Falcon*, 1941, directed by John Huston, starring Humphrey Bogart, Mary Astor, Peter Lorre, and Sydney Greenstreet. This is a good example of a new decade changing the type of movies filmed.
- *A Streetcar Named Desire*, 1951, directed by Elia Kazan, starring Vivien Leigh, Marlon Brando, and Kim Hunter. This movie shows how themes changed after World War II.
- *Darling*, 1965, directed by John Schlesinger, starring Julie Christie, Dirk Bogarde, and Laurence Harvey. This movie shows how themes changed after the second wave of feminism.

Assignment

The story begins at a critical junction. Jack and Suzie are in a waiting room of a doctor's office waiting for their best friend, Alec. Jack is Alec's next of kin as Alec is not willing to share any diagnostic results with any of his living relatives. Alec enters the waiting room and immediately goes to Suzie as the doctor calls Jack into his office.

The doctor tells Jack that Alec only has several months, possibly six, to live. When the disease gets intense, Alec will deteriorate very rapidly. Jack asks the doctor what the best thing is to do for him. The doctor is quiet for a moment and then he states that if he were Alec, he would want to go on one last fling. Jack leaves the doctor's office and Suzie asks him right away what the doctor said because Alec will not tell her anything.

Discuss the type of theme that this movie could have? How would you develop this movie synopsis for this theme?

3 Webster's Encyclopedic Unabridged Dictionary of the English Language. Rev. ed. (New York: Gramercy, 1996), 1471.

4 United States v. Paramount Pictures, Inc., 334 US 131 (1948).

2. What Is Genre and How Is It Determined?

Webster's Encyclopedic Unabridged Dictionary of the English Language defines genre as "a category of artistic, musical, or literary composition characterized by a particular style, form, or content."[5]

In other words, genre categorizes movies. Categorizing movies makes it easier for the viewer to discover what he or she likes and will want to see. Putting a movie into a particular genre or category does not diminish the quality of the movie by assuming that if it can be put into a genre, the movie is ordinary and lacks originality and creativity.

Genre consists of four elements or parts: character, story, plot and setting. An equation for remembering the genre is: Story (Action) + Plot + Character + Setting = Genre. This becomes an easy way to remember the elements of a genre.

The above elements of story, plot, setting, and character equal a specific category of movie. These elements are discussed regarding how their variations create a different category of movie.

Some genres may be as general as comedy but do not have sub-genres like comedy. The sub-genres of comedy differ from one another based on the fluctuations of the characters and the story.

Other genres are crime, war, Westerns, spy, adventure, science fiction, horror, fantasy, biography, and mystery. This is why this chapter is longer than the others because of the discussion of these variations.

Drama can be considered a genre, even though some critics do not consider it a genre because it is too general. If the movie elements are serious and cannot fit into a more limited genre, then it can be considered a drama.

Categorizing a movie indirectly assists in shaping the characters and the story of the movie. The shaping determines the plot and best setting to use.

Movies often have genres that overlap, such as adventure in a spy movie, or crime in a science fiction movie. But one genre is predominant.

Other movie labels cannot be considered genres. Film noir, thrillers, and action movies are not actually genres but a director's style, which will be discussed in a later chapter. They are considered director's style because their characteristics include cinematography and editing, which are not among the four elements that make up a genre. These labels reflect or accentuate the movie genre rather than defining the genre.

Likewise, musicals and animation are not considered genres but rather "treatments" as to how a particular movie genre is told, even though people, over generations, refer to these types of movies as genres.

You have to be very specific in the discussion of movie terminology, sticking within the particular definition of the terms. Some people will say that genres are labels that are given to stock movies, stating that these movies are routine. Being labeled in a genre is not a negative action.

Movies have their own personalities. Each movie is different. Having a movie labeled in a genre assists people to find a particular movie that they may be interested in watching. Many people like a specific genre or two and will only watch movies in those genres.

What People Like the Most about a Movie

People will state that a particular movie had a good plot or an intriguing story. What people are actually referring to is that they enjoyed the characters, the problems/conflict the characters got into, and how the characters got out of the problems and conflict.

People love a movie because they like to watch characters/people. How many people do you know who like to go to the mall, plaza, or beach and state that they like to people watch? How many people are nosey neighbors because they like to watch what is going on with the people around them?

People may like to watch crime movies or Westerns. They like characters within this particular type of story because of the amount of action or the time period setting. People may like Westerns because they wish they lived in the 19th century because it was considered a simpler time.

Let the Genres Begin

We will begin to discuss the different genres, and even the sub-genres, for certain genre types. I will give a hypothetical example of each so you will begin to see how different genres are formed.

Keep in mind with movie genre, it is the characters that make the movie, and this term is obvious enough that no explanation is needed.

The story is the situation that the characters are in and try to get out of, accomplish, conquer, or overcome. The story has a beginning, middle, and end. More discussion about those will be given in Chapter Three.

The plot is the outline or how the story is told. Remember when people state that they did not like the plot? What they are referring to is that they did not like the story. I will be referring to this concept over and over again throughout the book.

There are only a limited number of plots as the plot is a general outline for a story, like revenge. A particular plot describes how a story will begin, develop, and end. This type of story will have a different format than a plot such as man against nature or man versus the government.

In addition, as we progress through genres, we want to examine how the genre elements change.

You will be able to see that the background and actions of the characters change as the type of stories are different. The setting is dependent upon the story, but the plot remains the same.

I want to stress that we are going through the different genres so character and story development can be seen for each of the genres rather than just giving a general overview of the term genre. I want you to see how only certain elements are contained in a genre, and other elements outside of character, story, plot, and setting are not part of determining a genre.

Comedy Genre

We begin by discussing one of the most popular, general, and complicated genres—comedy.

The *Merriam-Webster Dictionary* defines comedy simply as "a play, movie, television program, novel, etc., that is meant to make people laugh."[6] We will discuss comedy in a little more detail than that.

Everybody likes a comedy because everybody likes to laugh and feel good. People like to watch a comedy after a bad day, because once the movie has ended, you can deal with the negativity of the day easier. This is why even horrendous comedy movies can end up making a profit.

The characters and story for a comedy hinge on three areas: the unexpected, the unusual, and repetition. These three areas will generally make people laugh. Generally, a comedy will have a happy ending. Even though some people will deny it, everybody likes a happy ending because it makes them feel good. This is why comedies are so popular.

The complicated part of the comedy genre is that there are different types or sub-genres of comedy; depending upon how outrageous and impossible the characters and story are in the movie. Keep in mind that the plot is general, and the setting can be set in any time or any place.

We will discuss the comedy genre in terms of the different sub-genres of comedies and how the characters and story vary per sub-genre.

Comedies run a gamut, ranging from very physical to nonsensical to subtle to dark. We will discuss the sub-genres in that order, using the same hypothetical example but varying it to show how the different comedy sub-genres will change the characters' personalities and actions and the story.

The sub-genres of comedy are slapstick, farce, satire, and dark. Any other genres are a variation of these four types. Comedy is actually a variation of physical action and ridicule. The only exception is screwball comedy.

Screwball comedy has many different traits that are outside of a genre. Screwball comedy, because it existed during the Great Depression, contains class conflict between the middle and lower classes and the upper class, along with other peculiarities that only existed during that time period.

Finally, "chick flicks" are generally comedy movies that star women. The *Urban Dictionary* defines chick flicks as "A film that indulges in the hopes and dreams of women and/or girls and has a happy, fuzzy, ridiculously unrealistic ending." No doubt the concept of chick flicks goes back to what was previously mentioned; people like a particular type of movie because of the characters in the movie.

Slapstick Comedy

The *Merriam-Webster Dictionary* defines slapstick as comedy that involves physical action (such as falling down or hitting people).[7] Slapstick comedy, because of the physical action, which becomes extreme at times, has unrealistic characters in an unbelievable story or possibly a story linked together by episodes of the main character's/protagonist's life.

The plot is an inner conflict that builds and ends with these various comedic episodes. The setting can be any time or place that best exemplifies the comic antics that the characters go through.

Let's take a look at an example that demonstrates these elements.

Jack is down on his luck. He helps a girl, Suzie, whose car broke down near where Jack works. He helps her, and then she leaves, but he cannot get her out of his mind.

Then he sees her in one of his classes. He is afraid to talk to her though. Every time he tries to go up to her, he either stumbles and falls or gets involved with helping someone with disastrous consequences. The last time someone asked him to hold onto one of the ropes of the theatre rigging system where the backdrops were attached, too many stage weights attached to the rigging resulted in Jack flying into the air because he did not let go of the rope.

As luck always has it in a slapstick comedy, Suzie is still driving the old broken down car. She breaks down again in almost the same locations as last time. Jack swallowed what little pride he had left, and went to help her. He got her car started, but she did not drive away immediately after getting it fixed but stayed to talk to Jack. They talk, kiss, and accidentally turn the outside sprinkler system on, getting soaking wet in the romantic conclusion.

From this example, you can see that slapstick comedy is all about the characters and the episodic situations that they get into, resulting in physical comedy. The plot is inner conflict where Jack, the protagonist, wants to turn his life around. This then becomes the story. The story has a climax between Jack and Suzie. The setting is a college campus.

Farce

The *Merriam-Webster Dictionary* defines farce as "a funny play or movie about ridiculous situations and events."[8]

Plot has more prominence in farce than in slapstick because there is a satirical story. In other words, the story concerns a topic that is ridiculed in an extreme way. We can adjust the last example quite easily to demonstrate this.

Jack and Suzie are college students, and Alec is a well-known actor coming to the campus to play a role in the theatrical production at the college. This event has been arranged so the college theatre department can make money. Jack takes a dislike to Alec, but Suzie finds him fascinating. Alec finds himself fascinating. Slapstick is shown by the over-the-top acting that Alec does.

Jack has a difficult time wondering why Alec is famous. Suzie soon finds disenchantment with Alec because he is only concerned about himself. Jack and Suzie and the other theatre majors decide to take the actions of the play to the extreme to humiliate and humble Alec.

In a water scene, where Alec is supposed to pantomime having water thrown on him, real water is used. This drives Alec into a hysterical rage, and he chases Jack and Suzie on stage, off the stage, around the theatre, and out the theatre doors. Alec winds up accidently knocking himself unconscious. Jack states that the most natural acting that Alec has done is being knocked out.

Next, Jack develops a hair-brained scheme so the theatre department can make money. Jack and Suzie make a list of the wealthiest men and women in the area. They invite as many of these wealthy people in the area to participate in an auction. There will be five male winners and five female winners. The prize is that they win Jack and Suzie for a day to act as their slaves.

You can see that a farce has more of a story than slapstick comedy. The plot has an inner conflict of the protagonists, Jack and Suzie, needing money. This creates a story where college theatre students try outrageous ways to make money to save the theatre department. The story ridicules colleges, actors, and theatres in general. The actions of the characters are very slapstick with physical comedy throughout the movie.

Satire

The *Merriam-Webster Dictionary* defines satire as "a way of using humor to show that someone or something is foolish, weak, bad, etc.: humor that shows the weaknesses or bad qualities of a person, government, society, etc."[9]

Satire is subtler than farce or slapstick in the actions of the characters. The plot develops an inner conflict, but the story is more realistic and may, at times, not even appear to be a comedy.

In this example, the setting can remain as a college campus.

Jack and Suzie, once again, are college students. Alec, though, is the instructor, who has a drinking problem, and he is directing a class that Jack and Suzie have to take as a requirement of their theatre major. Alec tries to convince the students that there is no right or wrong way to direct, act, or design. In his mind, theatre is all done with emotion. If it feels right, then do it. In order to help them understand and develop their talents as directors, Alec gives the same answer to any question Jack and Suzie ask: "If it feels right, then do it."

Jack struggles to try and comprehend what Alec's statement means. He does not understand why he has to go through four years of college if he just has to recognize what feels right. Jack asks Alec for more of a discussion on what feels right. Alec then tells him, "You'll know." This frustrates Jack even more because it does not take four years in college to put to use nine words that do not mean anything specific in regard to studying theatre. He questions the college administration as to why they are paying so much for Alec. The college administration retorts that Alec is one of the best in his field. Jack states that Alec teaches absolutely nothing of any value. The administration states, "That shows how good he is; you do not even realize the education you are receiving."

Defeated, Jack goes to see Suzie, his last hope. Suzie tells him not to be too quick to judge. Suzie states that she believes she understands what Alec is driving at with his ideas. Suzie tries to demonstrate the statements that Alec has mentioned. After a few hours Suzie becomes frustrated and states the both of them must go to see Alec.

After two hours with Alec, Jack and Suzie are delirious. Being delirious, they finally fathom what Alec means. They both run out of Alec's house and down the street shouting, "We have identified what it is!"

From this discussion of the characters and story, physical actions do not enter as a predominant element that they do in straight slapstick or farce. The satire is an obvious ridicule of theatre as a major and the type of people in theatre.

A more subtle satire would be Jack and Suzie acting as a clique and by being prima donnas. They mock a new theatre major, Alec, who wants to do a good job. Alec starts to develop his talent under strenuous and often humorous situations with consequences to the amazement of Jack and Suzie. But then he realizes what he has to give up for it. He quits for his own self-respect.

The above are two demonstrations of satire.

The first example, depending on the treatment, could become either a farce, if Jack's, Suzie's, or Alec's actions become too outrageous, exaggerated, and over-the-top, or it could become a satire. The line of demarcation between farce and satire are, as with anything that is analytical, left up to an individual's judgment. When does extreme satire become farce? A good way to judge farce or satire is how much unrealistic physical comedy is in the movie.

Dark Comedy or Black Comedy

Dictionary.com defines dark humor or black comedy as "in literature and drama, combining the morbid and grotesque with humor and farce to give a disturbing effect and convey the absurdity and cruelty of life."[10] [11]

Dark humor and black comedy are terms that make fun of or ridicule taboo topics like death. The characters are involved in a story that goes to the point of being grotesque and not being funny.

With this example of a college theatre as the setting, and the plot being the inner conflict of the main character, how can the characters and story become absurd, morbid, and grotesque when discussing the taboo topic of death? Quite easily actually!

Insecure about his acting ability and visibly showing this in public auditions, Jack does not obtain the role on stage that he desires, Henry V or "Hank 5," which is Jack's nickname for him. In order to relieve himself of his frustrations, Jack tortures and kills everyone who receives this part in the most brutally visual ways imaginable. He does this in hopes of eventually receiving this specific coveted role. Jack, though, is the only one who believes this role is so desirable and sought after.

Jack kills the first person who is given the role, Alec, by drawing and quartering him before he hangs him.

The second person to be given the role is Suzie, which really angers and infuriates Jack that a woman would get the role before him. This action adds absurdity to the story.

This is a dark humor movie rather than a serious movie because of the reasons, background, and extreme actions in the story. The characters act realistically based on their personalities, which are all unusual. The physical action is real so this scenario cannot be considered slapstick.

Screwball Comedy

This comedy sub-genre is named after a baseball pitch, the screwball, which was perfected by baseball pitcher Carl Hubbell in the 1930s. Screwball comedy only lasted from 1934, when the Great Depression was in full swing, to 1941, when World War II began.

Screwball comedy was based on reverse class snobbery where it is more noble to be poor than rich. The rich were portrayed as eccentric and wasteful fools. Romance is one of the key elements of screwball comedy. With the two classes of upper and lower or middle class working together, screwball comedies can be considered as recommending socialism. The story is a little different, but overall, it can be considered within the realm of satire because the current society was being ridiculed.

Screwball comedy also had the following attributes:

- The poor and middle class would go to the movies to see the rich get their comeuppance. This is why movies were one of the few industries of the period that made a profit. People felt a passion of hate toward the upper class because of the mess lower classes assumed the upper class made of the economy.
- Many of the most famous movie stars of the period appeared in screwball comedies.
- People went to the movies to see the elegant clothes, cars, and furniture, so they could wish they had those items.

Any referral to a movie as a screwball comedy after 1941 is inaccurate, even if it is a re-make of a movie released during the 1934-1941 period. A re-make does not have the same relevancy, power, or passion as the original movie.

A contemporary screwball-type comedy generally is fast paced with an eccentric character, but it does not have the class snobbery. Any class snobbery in the movie does not have the contemptable hatred toward the upper class as it did these movies during the Great Depression. The emotional rage cannot be duplicated.

Romantic Comedy

Dictionary.com defines romantic comedy as "a light and humorous movie, play, etc., whose central plot is a happy love story."[12]

Romantic comedy is contained in most comedies as a sub-story, such as *The Front Page*, which has an underlying romantic story of Hildy wanting to marry his fiancée and leave newspaper reporting. However, the overriding story of the movie concerns reporters and editors doing anything in order to get the story.

Comic romance is a big element in screwball comedy also, but other story lines are more dominant.

Can you think of a movie that has the primary story line as being a romantic relationship? If you can, how did you like the movie?

Comedy Conclusion

Comedy is varied and complex. You can see how the stories, along with the personalities and actions of the characters, change, developing different sub-genres of the comedy being expressed. All comedy stems from either slapstick or satire.

Let's move on to a new genre.

Crime Genre

Staying with the letter "C," let's move on to the crime genre.

The *Merriam-Webster Dictionary* defines crime as "an act or the commission of an act that is forbidden or the omission of a duty that is commanded by a public law and that makes the offender liable to punishment by that law" or more simply "a grave offense especially against morality."[13] The definition gives us a lot to work with, so we will do our best to bring it into focus.

The first point is that every aspect of the crime genre is dramatic, so the elements are quite different than a comedy. The setting for crime genre can be any location in the world and any year, because crime is something that has always existed in society. We will try to narrow this down for our example.

The plot is an inner conflict for the criminal to succeed or for the "good guy" to succeed. The story is a series of developing incidents where the criminal or the "good guy" is the protagonist and a conflict has to be overcome. The characters develop from the story and plot.

Let's demonstrate two examples with Jack being the protagonist in both situations. In the first situation, Jack is a criminal and the second one Jack is the "good guy."

First situation: Jack is a nice, helpful individual at the beginning of the movie. He soon finds that he has to help a friend, Suzie, get out of a jam because she owes a lot of money to a gambling boss, Alec. Jack goes and begins to negotiate honestly in regard to paying Suzie's debt. Alec laughs at him and is going to throw him out. Jack, even though he is a nice guy, has a very bad temper. This often is the situation in the crime genre. Jack becomes extremely angry with Alec laughing at him, and he kills Alec.

Alec's men come in and Jack tells them he is their new boss. The men don't like it, but they reserve any action for a later time. Suzie likes the new Jack and wants to be his girl. Suzie is aroused by the violence in Jack and cannot keep her hands off him.

Jack soon becomes more successful than Alec ever was, but he begins to become too egotistical. With his ego getting in the way, Jack makes a mistake when trying to take over a gambling casino. Jack is killed and the men kill Suzie. The most jealous, vindictive, right-hand man in the gang takes over the gambling empire.

Stories in the crime genre are often about people seeking power. Usually, the criminals want control over the city where the story takes place. Generally, they want to be in charge of the drug trade, gambling, liquor (depending upon the year), or they want to rise up in the family or gang. There are always periods of violent action with the protagonist trying to reach his/her goal.

Second situation: Jack is a police detective in a large city like New York City or Los Angeles. Jack is a hardworking, honest detective. He is dedicated to his job and his partner, Alec. Jack spends most of his free time with Alec and Alec's family. Alec is murdered. Even though he wasn't put on the case, because they were partners and friends, Jack spends his free time investigating who murdered Alec. During his investigation he meets Suzie. Suzie knew Alec and considered him a friend. Suzie asks if she can help with looking into the murder. Jack, after some convincing, agrees.

Suzie and Jack start to become close during the investigation, and Jack falls in love with her. This is often a foreshadowing as to how the story is going to end. After a few dead ends and blocked paths in the investigation, Jack picks up some information that leads him down an unsuspected path. Jack finds that Suzie was a little more than a friend to Alec, so Suzie has an ulterior motive for assisting Jack. Jack discovers that Suzie murdered Alec and was going to kill Jack, too. Jack arrests Suzie for Alec's murder.

These are the elements and formats of the crime genre. The crime can be different than murder. Crimes encompass a wide variety of different actions. The main characters do not have to be crime bosses or police detectives, but they generally have a similar background. Very seldom do they lead a life like a factory worker or office employee. This is one reason why the crime genre is so popular. People want to watch characters that lead exciting lives different from theirs.

The stories in the crime genre are similar to the aforementioned two examples where the crime is more than a speeding ticket and provides an interesting and exciting story. The plot can be an inner conflict, once again, of the protagonist, and the setting is usually in the United States or Europe in modern times.

Western Genre

Because of the similarities between the Western and crime genres, I have included back-to-back discussions of the two genres.

The *Merriam-Webster Dictionary* defines Western simply as "of or relating to the American West."[14] Keeping this in mind, we will begin by discussing the setting.

The setting provides the major difference between the crime genre and the Western genre. Instead of the characters and story occurring in the 1930s or the 1990s, the time for a Western is in the early to late 19th century or anytime through the 1820s to 1890s. Once the 20th century arrives, except for the beginning years, the feeling of the Old West is gone, which brings up the other aspect of the setting that defines the Western genre. The Western genre takes place in the West. Depending upon the year, the West could be Ohio in the 1820s, Missouri in the 1850s, or Nevada in the 1880s.

The main character or protagonist is an individualist, who rides into town for a specific reason, or he may run into trouble while in town, or he may be hired to do something like blaze a trail West. The characters and the stories are straightforward. The interest is the developing story and the action-filled problems that the protagonist faces as he tries to accomplish what he set out to do.

The plot can still be one of inner conflict as the protagonist tries to accomplish the specific goal, quell the trouble in town, or overcome the obstacles of nature as the main character blazes the trail West.

An example of the Western genre has Jack being the individualist, loner riding into town. He has come to town to avenge the death of his partner. Outside of the setting, the same type of character and story could be used in the crime genre. While Jack begins to ask questions about what happened to his partner, he falls into the middle of a range war; a typical Western story, between two ranches over the grazing rights of land. Alec owns the one ranch, and Suzie (a woman) owns the other, which is a rarity in the West.

Jack gets to know Suzie as his inquiries continue. He begins a relationship with her. During the relationship, Jack gives Suzie a helping hand in the range war. Alec is totally evil, underhanded, and despicable in his actions. Westerns, even more contemporary ones, have an outright bad person like Alec. You can see this in crime genre movies also.

Jack defeats Alec in the range war, and in the process, finds that Alec also killed Jack's partner. In the Old West, there can only be one climax to the story. Jack and Alec shoot it out; Alec is killed, and Jack and Suzie fall in love.

War Genre

The *Merriam-Webster Dictionary* defines war as "a state or period of fighting between countries or groups."[15] With this definition being direct, we can discuss the genre in the same manner. The war genre is straightforward because the movie is very limited in its parameters.

The setting and the year is very specific regarding the year and the location. If the movie takes place from the United States' perspective, World War I would be from 1917 to 1918; World War II would be from 1941 to 1945; and the Korean Conflict, Vietnam War, Desert Storm, and other Middle East conflicts follow the same procedure. The locations would be an area where the war occurred or in the United States to concentrate on how the home front was coping.

The plot is the inner conflict with dealing with war. The characters and story are based on a battle, trying to obtain overall victory at some point of the war, dealing with losing, dealing with death, dealing with fighting, being a prisoner, or coping at the home front or a location where the fighting is not taking place.

World War II encompasses the war genre. Jack is a soldier, who is a married teacher with two children. He is drafted by the United States shortly after World War II started late in 1941. Jack was told by his wife, Suzie, not to volunteer for any extra missions so he could come home alive to his family when the war is over. Of course, this is not going to be true because a war movie has to have a daring mission.

After being in Europe for about a year and losing many battles, Jack becomes frustrated because he knows the war is not going to end soon. Suzie dreads each day because of the emptiness in her life without Jack. To her, each day never appears to end. She is stressed because she has a continuous challenge to make ends meet.

Jack and seven other men are given a chance to go on a dangerous mission to blow up a German stronghold and capture a high-ranking German officer. These men are asked to go on this mission because of their intelligence and personalities. If they succeed in this mission, the war will likely be over quicker than expected, because of the information they will receive from this German officer. Jack remembers that his wife told him never to volunteer, but he knows he only has once choice. He volunteers. Suzie gets a feeling of foreboding and is suddenly afraid something bad is going to happen. She starts to become distant to her friends and even her children.

Jack goes on the mission. Everything is timed perfectly. The fortress is blown up and the German officer is captured. However, the trip back to the Allied lines did not go as planned. Half the men are killed, Jack is wounded, and the German officer is killed.

Suzie's feeling of foreboding becomes so great that, at one point, she passes out with anxiety. The Christmas holidays are near, and Suzie is persuaded to take the children to church. As the service begins, Jack walks into the church and joins Suzie and the children. The story ends happily, but with a cost. In order to give the story a more realistic feel, the protagonist is not totally successful with what he had set out to do.

Spy Genre

The *Merriam-Webster Dictionary* defines spy as "to watch secretly usually for hostile purposes" or "to search or look for intensively."[16] I want to give two short definitions to emphasize the spy genre because it is a combination of watching and searching, but I do not want it to get confused with the next genre of adventure.

The spy genre sounds like it could cross over to the previous genres already discussed. But only the setting and the plot can be standard. The setting could be the same as the war, Western, or crime genres, but it does not make it a war, Western, or crime genre. You have to remember that the story makes the genre because it controls everything else.

In the spy genre, the main character generally works under an assumed identity in order to find something or destroy something of harm controlled by a nemesis. As in past genres, the plot is the inner conflict of the protagonist. In this situation, he or she has a strong inner conflict to succeed at what he or she is assigned to act upon.

Thus, if the movie has any of the aforementioned characteristics but takes place during World War II, the movie is primarily a spy movie rather than a war movie. Remember, the setting does not determine the genre but the story does. The story is interconnected to the characters and the plot. The setting helps add the must-needed background and specificity to the movie, but it is not as interconnected as the other three genres.

In recent times, a male of the strong virile type plays the protagonist spy. So, we will demonstrate that this does not always have to be that way in a movie. We will take a woman, named Suzie, who is the spy protagonist. We will set the example during World War II. Unlike Jack in the war genre discussion, Suzie is chosen because of her background in languages and her photographic memory, giving her the ability to memorize lists of facts immediately. She is requested to go behind enemy lines as a civilian and obtain data that will debilitate the enemy thus giving the Allies the advantage and shortening the war by possibly years.

In order to be able to do this, and to prepare her mentally for the task, she is set to train for three weeks with an Army officer named Jack. Jack is very skeptical that Suzie will be able to pull the task off. Jack states that it is not because she is a woman, but the movie viewers know that her being a woman is exactly the reason.

Jack begins a rigorous training program just to say that he told her so. However, Suzie really masters everything Jack throws at her. After about a week, Jack sees this and starts to admire her strength and fortitude. Jack makes the training less rigorous because he only trains her to get behind enemy lines, get back to the Allied lines, and how to mentally survive torture. By the end of the three weeks, they begin to fall in love with each other, and Jack feels he should accompany her, but his command says that is impossible.

The time has arrived for Suzie to go. The French underground has managed to get her a clerical job where she can do some travelling including going to Normandy. Rather abruptly, Suzie plans a trip to Normandy. She studies the land and is able to secretly catch a glimpse of German maps showing where their military strength is in and around Normandy. Suzie rushes and gets the information off to the Allies before she is captured by the Germans. The Allies receive Suzie's information, but they cannot help Suzie. The Germans find her guilty of being a spy and she is executed.

Can you see the difference between this example and the war genre example? Both have the same setting of World War II, but the spy genre example has a non-soldier searching for secret information, while the war genre had a group of soldiers going on a mission that was not secret. The war mission was behind enemy lines and in the war zone where the fighting was occurring. The spy genre does not occur in the war zone where there was fighting.

Do you see the differences in the stories?

The spy story has a lot less emotion and love between the main characters. The spy story has more suspense as Suzie is hunting for information. She is becoming involved in several tight situations where she barely misses getting caught by the Nazis. The war genre story has the one climatic battle that the whole conflict was moving toward.

Most of the time these two genres do not become this similar but these two examples make it easier to see the differences in the two genres.

Adventure Genre

The *Merriam-Webster Dictionary* defines adventure as "an undertaking usually involving danger and unknown risks" that is "an exciting or remarkable experience."[17] From this definition, you can see that adventure is an action movie that overlaps with the spy genre with danger, risks, and excitement.

Both the adventure and spy genres can have exotic settings. The stories are normally about a person or group of people searching for something. During the journey of searching, dangerous situations are overcome by the main characters. The protagonist may end up getting involved in fighting to overcome social or moral injustices in the exotic location where he or she has journeyed.

The difference between this genre and the spy genre is, once again, the story. The spy genre has a story where something is searched for secretively, and the information itself contains secret information. This story has suspense based on timing and near misses.

The adventure genre's suspense is found in the action and the chance that the protagonist may get killed without the espionage. The protagonist is an adventurer rather than a government employee.

Being bigger than life, the adventure genre contains a lot of explosive action throughout the movie. Remember that the story treatment, character background, and character development are big differentiations and distinctions that separate genres. The plot and the setting are also different between genres, and are reflective of the story and the types of characters.

Science Fiction Genre

Science fiction is linked to the previous genres of crime, Westerns, war, spy, and adventure by the basic theme. However, the genre elements are totally different.

The *Merriam-Webster Dictionary* defines science fiction as "fiction dealing principally with the impact of actual or imagined science on society or individuals or having a scientific factor as an essential orienting component."[18] An example of science fiction is time travel, which has and is a popular topic.

Quite often, science fiction has a setting that takes place in the future. In this way, if the producer wants to comment on a particular problem in current society, the producer can set the problem in the future. The producer appears critical about the problem but not about the current society. The outcome of that problem, if it continues, shows how the future will look.

For science fiction, we can still stay with the plot of inner conflict, which can always be the plot, because a conflict is needed. The characters and the story can be the same as any other genre with variations, as we will demonstrate in the example.

In our example, Jack and Suzie, along with several hundred other people, are fed up with the crime and violence that exists where they live. No specific location is mentioned, so it can be anywhere in the world or universe.

In this movie, many of Jack and Suzies' group are engineers who work endlessly to build several space ships that to travel to a new galaxy, away from the crime and chaos. Researchers in this group toil endlessly to find a new galaxy that is livable for humans. Together they all dream of pioneering and developing this new world so there is no violence and everyone can live in harmony.

By seeing the people's action of building space ships, the audience learns that the time is the future.

The space ships are finally finished and they are sent off. They find and arrive in the new world that is named New Earth. The people set up a colony and draft laws so there is no anarchy. Everything is great for two generations. The people live in harmony and enjoy each day to the utmost.

However, one day, someone is found dead and robbed. Everyone is left shocked. Because so much time has passed without violence, the police are unprepared. But they review the crime scene, and conclude that it was murder.

Since they have never investigated a murder, they are unsure what should they do to find the murderer and how should they to go about doing it. They arrive at a procedure and find the murderer. The murder was an accident. The murderer was surprised as everyone else. The people realize a murder or accidental death can always happen, so the society has to be prepared and set up to handle it. Even though the story is fantastical in many ways, it can still make comments and raise questions about society and morality.

Science fiction genre, like any genre, can cross over at some point or points to another genre. This example crossed over to the crime genre. However, to determine the main genre, review the story, characters, plot, and setting together. In this situation, these elements are most geared toward the science fiction genre.

Fantasy Genre

The *Merriam-Webster Dictionary* defines fantasy as "something that is produced by the imagination: an idea about doing something that is far removed from normal reality."[19]

In other words, a fantasy movie has no limits. The setting could be anywhere at any time with characters who appear and act in any way the script writer wants. The story could be about anything. So let's stick with one constant, the plot. The plot will be inner conflict.

According to Wikipedia, fantasy stays away from scientific and macabre story aspects, so it does not become a piece of science fiction or horror. You can see how all three genres: science fiction, fantasy, and horror are similar but different.

What would a fantasy example be like?

A group of misfits are given a task by a wizard to find the perfect person. They must do this in order to save their friend, who is terminally ill and will die shortly. The wizard tells them that their friend is not terminally ill but under an evil spell that he can break. The perfect person is the wizard's fee for breaking the spell. The characters are Jack, Suzie, and Alec, who are misfits because they are the outcasts from their home village, which is in a fictional country. The wizard gives them a clue to look where no one has looked or would think of looking.

Jack, Suzie, and Alec think that the perfect place to find the perfect person is in a graveyard because nobody would think of looking there. But how would the perfect person appear in a graveyard? After searching through several cemeteries, they become frustrated because they find nothing unusual and do not know what the wizard was talking about. They finally find a cemetery where they can enter a new world that is built upon their imaginations. Using their imaginations mean, as they discuss a trait or physical appearance, they can build the person using their minds. What they imagine can become reality.

Using their imaginations, they begin to discuss what the perfect person would look like and act. What would the person's personality be like? They cannot decide because the traits that they imagined as a perfect person are foreign to them. Finally, they start talking about themselves, and what they like and do not like.

After a lengthy conversation that continues for days, Suzie stands up and yells that she has the answer. She states they should make three lists of their best physical and mental traits. That will be the perfect person. The perfect person is within them as it is within all people. They compile the perfect person using their imaginations and take it to the wizard.

Suzie explains to the wizard with the assistance of Jack and Alec that the perfect person was within them as it is within all people. The wizard states that they found the answer to the clue. As such, they are also able to break the spell over their friend. The spell is broken, and the four leave and live happily ever after.

You are only limited by your imagination. A wonderful theme can come from any genre.

Horror Genre

The *Merriam-Webster Dictionary* defines horror as "the quality of something that causes feelings of fear, dread, and shock: the horrible or shocking quality or character of something." A horror show is "something that is difficult to deal with or watch because it is so bad, unpleasant, etc."[20]

The setting regarding where the movie takes place can be instrumental in a horror movie. Many times, horror movies take place in a historical area with big, old houses that hold many secrets. Secrets provide the basis of a story as the house is supposedly haunted because something gruesome happened there many years ago. However, the setting may not be unusual, but it can be a typical small town or city just like the one where you live.

The plot, once again, is inner conflict. The main character, Suzie, inherits the house, and she is determined—to the point of becoming obsessed—to prove that there is no such thing as a haunted house. However, she takes her boyfriend, Jack, with her to the house. After they become frightened by unearthly occurrences in the house, Jack asks his friend, Alec, to join them at the house to find a solution to what is going on.

Alec states that in order to make it a clean, healthy house again, they have to discover the problem and solve it. In order to do this, Alec recommends doing a séance. The three of them enter a room late in the evening and try to contact a spirit to identify the problem. They find, at one point, that the house was owned by a slave trader or human trafficker. Down in the basement, many bodies were buried.

Suzie cannot stand thinking that a relative was a human trafficker and nothing can really be done to solve this problem. The house was owned by an evil man who is suffering in the spirit world because of his past actions. Jack thinks that the only cure to these past heinous actions is to burn the house down, which would cremate the bodies that were buried in the basement and possibly put them at peace.

Suzie does not agree with that action, but Alec agrees with Jack in order to find a cure for the haunting. Possibly, after the burning, Suzie can build a different house. Suzie starts to act in an irrational manner, like she is becoming her past relative, who was the slaver. Alec and Jack burn the house. Suzie becomes completely enraged and has to be restrained until the house is completely burned down.

Once the house has finished burning, Suzie no longer acts like she is possessed. The whole area becomes quiet. Suzie speculates that they just need drive away from it. The three of them drive away.

The horror genre brings fear, and fear generally brings thrills and suspense. With a suspenseful scene, people like to scare themselves. The theme can always be "search for the truth," rather than "do not be afraid of the unknown."

Drama Genre

If a movie does not fit in one of the aforementioned genre categories, then it is a drama.

The *Merriam-Webster Dictionary* defines drama as "a play, movie, television show, or radio show that is about a serious subject and is not meant to make the audience laugh" and "a composition in verse or prose intended to portray life or character or to tell a story usually involving conflicts and emotions through action and dialogue."[21]

The four elements of the drama genre have to be serious, portray life, tell a story, and the characters have to have an inner conflict that brings out emotions at different times throughout the story. These are all points that we have been discussing with the other genres. The characters and the story are general, like everyday people and situations.

Somebody is dying, something has to be obtained, or something has to be accomplished are the three common stories for dramas. Jack is an accomplished musician, who is going to be playing at Carnegie Hall, and he finds out that he has a fatal illness after passing out during a rehearsal. Or, Jack lived in the slums and a teacher noticed something in him that could be cultivated. Jack becomes a renowned doctor, scientist, or mathematician. The movie covers Jack's obstacles to achieve what is necessary for him to being on the road toward a renowned career.

Or, Suzie risks everything to find a cure for a disease that is killing many thousands of people on a Caribbean island. The viewer often knows what is going to happen but often the characters and their development is what makes a drama interesting.

The story is relatively simple, the plot is inner conflict, and the setting is inconsequential because the characters make the movie.

Did you find *Cyrano de Bergerac* to be a drama? *Cyrano de Bergerac* had a firm foundation in unrequited love, a very romantic element in the story. But Cyrano's inner conflict of his feelings of inadequacies in his personal appearance, while being overconfident in other areas, present love in a dramatic genre.

Action, Thriller, Suspense Thriller, Biography, Film Noir, Neo Noir, and Mystery

Action, thriller, suspense-thriller, biography, film noir, neo noir, and mystery are terms that are often referred to as different genres. However, none of these are genres. They do not contain just the four basic elements of a genre—no matter how much people insist that they do. They contain the genre elements and other elements, like cinematography, that are not part of a genre.

Writers, educators, critics, historians, and others have stated that the above terms developed into being named a genre and that they can be accepted as a genre over time. How many of you heard or read the terms action genre, film noir genre, or suspense thriller genre? Just because they have been referred to by these terms, over the years, does not make them honorary genres. These terms, by themselves, still have the same meaning even if they have been named genres.

Most of these terms refer to specific cinematography when shooting the movie, or they refer to the way the movie was edited.

Action, thrillers, and suspense thrillers all have similar types of action in them. Adventure, spy, crime, war, and Westerns could all be action movies or thrillers or suspense thrillers. Action, thrillers, and suspense thrillers do not touch upon the four elements that make up a genre.

Film noir and neo noir are predominantly crime movies that have certain cinematography. They overlap both in the construction and production aspects of making a movie.

Film noir means "black film." Film noir has many scenes occurring at night with many gritty, seedy city shots. The character types in film noir are loners and schemers, but they are reflective of the types of characters in crime movies.

Detour is a good example of film noir regarding the characters like Al and Vera. The voice-over narration of the protagonist describing the forward action, using black and white film, and many scenes occurring at night are examples of film noir. But voice-over narration, being in black and white, and a lot of the movie occurring at night does not determine the genre. The jaded characters, story, and plot of murder defines the movie as a member of the crime genre. The night scenes and voice-over narration are a directorial style. These decisions are characteristics that distinguish it as film noir.

Neo noir is the new noir for the later 20th and 21st centuries when most movies are made in color. The genres could be crime, science fiction, or drama but the cinematography is dark, gritty, and symbolic, similar in many respects to film noir.

Mystery refers to the way the story is shaped. Most mysteries are concerned with who stole something or who murdered someone. Most mysteries belong to the crime genre where the story and the editing keep the audience guessing until the final minutes of the movie.

Biography refers to a nonfiction movie that is about a historical or living person. The background, character, and setting of the movie may determine what other genre a biography might belong to. If the person is a war hero, the movie would be of the war genre; if the person was a criminal or detective, the movie would fit the crime genre, and so forth.

Documentary

Documentary, according to *Dictionary.com*, refers to movies and television features based on or re-creating an actual event, era, life story, etc., that purports to be factually accurate and contains no fictional elements.[22]

Sheila Curran Bernard,[23] author of *Documentary Storytelling*, defines documentaries as:

> Documentaries bring viewers into new worlds and experiences through the presentation of factual information about real people, places, and events, generally — but not always — portrayed through the use of actual images and artifacts. But factuality alone does not define documentary films; it's what the filmmaker does with those factual elements, weaving them into an overall narrative that strives to be as compelling as it is truthful and is often greater than the sum of its parts.

From these two definitions, documentaries are a separate movie entity that is unto itself.

Final Thought

We covered a lot of area in discussing different genres. Even though genres are only considered labels for movies, the four elements of a genre are the basis of any movie. Besides categorizing, genres indirectly shape the movie's characters and story.

Character, story, plot, and setting are how a movie is constructed. From this construction, the specific theme that is created by the screenwriter and the director can be realized and understood by the viewer.

The other chapters in the construction of a movie go into more detail and dissect these elements in order for a better understanding of the scope of these elements and how the theme of the movie is realized.

Further Viewing

With the completion of this chapter, the movies to watch that that are excellent examples of different genres are:

- *It Happened One Night*, 1934, directed by Frank Capra, starring Clark Gable and Claudette Colbert. This is an excellent example of screwball comedy. It is considered the first screwball comedy, and it won five Academy Awards for Best Picture, Best Actor, Best Actress, Best Director, and Best Adapted Screenplay.
- *They Were Expendable*, 1945, directed by John Ford, starring Robert Montgomery and John Wayne. This is a good example of the war genre. It is set during the beginning of World War II and demonstrates how the United States lost the war with dignity.
- *All About Eve*, 1950, directed by Joseph L. Mankiewicz, starring Bette Davis, Anne Baxter, and George Sanders. This is an excellent example of the drama genre.
- *Goldfinger*, 1964, directed by Guy Hamilton, starring Sean Connery, Gert Fröbe, and Honor Blackman. This is an excellent example of the spy genre that became popular as well as the gadgets that came along with it.
- *Raiders of the Lost Ark*, 1981, directed by Steven Spielberg, starring Harrison Ford as Indiana Jones. This is a good example of the adventure genre.

Assignment

Jack is a school teacher, which is a job he loves. He wants to be the best teacher possible and serve his students well. Because of his desire to serve his students, he has a disdain for the school administration when they want to cut back on the education process while serving themselves with excessive raises. In addition, Jack had a bad family life when growing up. He is rather cold to his mother because of his upbringing. His mother was domineering to him and his father died at an early age. Jack's bad family life is a big reason why he became a teacher. He wanted to make sure his students were treated better in school than he was at home.

Based on the above introduction, what genre or genres could this movie idea be developed into?

5 Webster's Encyclopedic Unabridged Dictionary, 591.

6 "Comedy," Merriam-Webster Dictionary, http://www.merriam-webster.com/dictionary/comedy.

7 "Slapstick," Merriam-Webster Dictionary, http://www.merriam-webster.com/dictionary/slapstick.

8 "Farce," Merriam-Webster Dictionary, http://www.merriam-webster.com/dictionary/farce.

9 "Satire," Merriam–Webster Dictionary, http://www.merriam-webster.com/dictionary/satire.

10 "Dark Humor," Dictionary.com, http://www.dictionary.com/browse/dark-humor?s=t.

11 "Black Comedy, Dictionary.com, http://www.dictionary.com/browse/black-comedy?s=t.

12 "Romantic Comedy," Dictionary.com, http://www.dictionary.com/browse/romantic-comedy?s=t.

13 "Crime," Merriam-Webster Dictionary, http://www.merriam-webster.com/dictionary/crime.html.

14 "Western," Merriam-Webster Dictionary, http://www.merriam-webster.com/dictionary/western.html.

15 "War," Merriam-Webster Dictionary, http://www.merriam-webster.com/dictionary/war.html.

16 "Spy," Merriam-Webster Dictionary, http://www.merriam-webster.com/dictionary/spy.

17 "Adventure," Merriam-Webster Dictionary, http://www.merriam-webster.com/dictionary/adventure.

18 "Science Fiction," Merriam-Webster Dictionary, http://www.merriam-webster.com/dictionary/science %20fiction.

19 "Fantasy," Merriam-Webster Dictionary, http://www.merriam-webster.com/dictionary/fantasy.

20 "Horror," Merriam-Webster Dictionary, http://www.merriam-webster.com/dictionary/horror.

21 "Drama," Merriam-Webster Dictionary, http://www.merriam-webster.com/dictionary/drama.

22 "Movies," Dictionary.com, http://www.dictionary.com/browse/movies?s=t.

23 Sheila Curran Bernard, "Documentary Storytelling: Creative Nonfiction on Screen," 3rd ed., (Burlington: Taylor & Francis, 2011).

3. What Are the Mechanics of Story and Plot?

InPoint, the online production resource at Pacific Cinémathèque, defines narrative structure in the following way: "Narrative structure is about two things: the content of a story and the form used to tell the story. Two common ways to describe these two parts of narrative structure are story and plot."[24]

In other words, narrative structure is the way the story and plot are utilized in a movie. In the previous chapter, we discussed the format for stories based on the genre. Plot was just referred to as inner conflict. We will now take the story and plot, discussing them in general terms without a specific genre in mind.

The narrative structure, as the term suggests, is the structural framework for a movie. The story is the action of the movie, and the plot is how the story is told. The narrative structure can be either linear or nonlinear. Linear narrative structure is a movie that moves in chronological order. Nonlinear structure is a movie that begins in the middle, also referred to as "in medias res." The story is told in flashbacks that proceed to the present day.

The formula for narrative structure so the parts and the function are easy to remember is: Story (**A**ction) + **P**lot = **N**arrative Structure.

So, if this is a complete overview of narrative structure, why is it so important that a whole chapter is devoted to it? If the movie didn't have any framework, would it make sense?

The framework provides the characters with something to accomplish and grow. Otherwise, they would have no beginning, middle, and end. Time would be meaningless to them. As pointed out above, time is one of the most meaningful parts of the narrative structure.

In order to discuss the narrative structure with meaningful detail, we have to discuss the two parts of the narrative structure, the story and the plot. We will discuss the plot first, given that the plot determines how the story is going to be told.

The Plot

The *Merriam-Webster Dictionary* defines plot as "a series of events that form the story in a novel, movie, etc."[25] Previously, we discussed only one type of plot: inner conflict. However, at this point, let's expand the discussion of the plot. Many people have theorized the number of different plots, each arriving at a different number of plots.

Ipl2 (Internet Public Library) addressed this statement in a Special Collections article entitled "The 'Basic' Plots in Literature."[26] In the ipl2 article, four people are discussed and the number of plots that they have come up with based on their own theory. Each of their theories purports different reasoning as to their specific numbers of basic plots. Foster-Harris in "The Basic Patterns of Plot", contends that there are three basic patterns of plot. IPL volunteer librarian Jessamyn West says there are seven plots. Ronald B. Tobias in "20 Master Plots", proposes twenty basic plots. Georges Polti in "The Thirty-Six Dramatic Situations", translated by Lucille Ray, states there are 36 plots.

Based on the aforementioned the number of plots range from three to seven to 20 to 36. There is no specific number of plots. However, if you review their plot lists, how many plots are similar?

Ronald Tobias' 20 plots list contains two plots referred to as love and forbidden love.[27] What is the difference between love and forbidden love? The plot of love can cover all love. In Polti's list of 36 plots, the plots are very specific, such as slaying of a kinsman unrecognized.[28]

A plot should be general in order to not limit the story. So, overall, we will consider 10 basic plots besides the general plot of inner conflict. The 10 plots are: quest, pursuit, rescue, revenge, the riddle, underdog, temptation, transformation, love, and discovery. Each plot is different enough to yield different action in the story.

Any more than these 10 plots and inner conflict will narrow the scope of the plot. The narrower the scope of the plot, the more restricted the action of the story.

Plots, though, do stand alone because they fuel the story. But alone, they are of no value. So at this point, let's take a look at the definition and parts of the story. Once the story has been defined, we will demonstrate how the plot fuels the story. Then we can discuss the narrative structure or the framework of the movie.

The Story

The *Merriam-Webster Dictionary* defines story as "an account of incidents or events."[29]

The story or the account of the events can be split up into six parts:

- The *exposition* is the beginning of the movie where the main characters of the movie are introduced and the viewer finds out something about the characters.
- The *complication* is the conflict that the protagonist must face, struggle with, and resolve by the end of the movie.
- The *rising action* is a series of sequences of action where the protagonist experiences advances and setbacks, moving toward the resolution of the conflict.
- The *climax* is the high point of the movie where the protagonist, based on the knowledge gained from the rising action, determines what the final action needs to be taken in order to resolve the conflict.
- The *falling action* ties up or resolves any minor loose story ends.
- The *denouement* is the ending of the movie.

We will diagram these six parts into more specific and familiar detail, so the parts form a continuous flow:

- The exposition and conflict form the beginning of the story.
- The rising action and the climax form the middle of the story, and
- The falling action and the resolution form the end of the story.

Now that we have a diagram for the story and a list of plots, let's see how the plot fuels the story to establish the narrative structure. We will use *The Front Page* and *Cyrano de Bergerac* as examples to demonstrate the construction of the framework for movies.

Examples of the Construction of Movie Framework

Using the two aforementioned plots, love and pursuit, we will analyze the story in *The Front Page*. How do the plots develop within the scene sequences of the story?

Do you remember the specific scenes from each of the six elements of the story and at what point the movie moves forward to the next element?

Exposition – The beginning of the movie introduces the viewer to the three main characters in the movie: newspaper reporter, Hildy Johnson; newspaper editor, Walter Burns, and Hildy's fiancée, Peggy Grant.

Complication – While Hildy wants to get married, Walter tries to persuade Hildy not to get married but remain a reporter for the newspaper.

Rising Action –

- Hildy goes to the court house press room and becomes involved with the story of the hanging of Earl Williams.
- Earl Williams escapes, and Hildy uses his honeymoon money to bribe someone for the story on what happened (moving forward with a possible set back).
- Hildy hides Earl Williams.
- Hildy and Walter get arrested, and Peggy breaks off the engagement.

Climax – Hildy and Walter are released and Hildy proposes to Peggy again.

Falling Action – Walter lets Hildy go and gives Hildy his watch as a wedding present. Hildy leaves.

Denouement – Walter calls the police to have Hildy arrested for stealing his watch.

Remembering the questions that were asked when discussing the story of *The Front Page*, how would a similar analysis be done for *Cyrano de Bergerac*? The plots are love and inner conflict in *Cyrano de Bergerac*. How do the plots develop the scene sequences of the story?

Exposition – Introduced to Cyrano, who is both a writer and swordsman, and Roxane is introduced.

Complication – Cyrano states to his friend that he loves Roxane, but he will not tell her because of his nose. Roxane tells Cyrano that she loves Christian.

Rising Action – The series of sequences leading to the climax:

- Cyrano befriends Christian at the request of Roxane, because she loves Christian (moving forward).
- Cyrano tells Christian that Roxane loves him.
- Cyrano helps Christian write a letter to Roxane.
- Christian states that he does not need Cyrano's help any longer (moving forward). Cyrano hides behind a bush and helps Christian. Cyrano gives an impassioned speech but Christian kisses Roxane (set back).
- Christian is ordered out to battle.
- Roxane visits Christian. Christian realizes Cyrano loves Roxane. Christian volunteers for a dangerous mission before Cyrano can proclaim his love to Roxane (set back).
- Before Christian dies, Cyrano states that Roxane chose him (moving forward).
- Roxane joins a convent. Cyrano visits Roxane at her convent each week for 14 years (moving forward and set back).

Climax – Cyrano is ambushed and run down by a carriage. He asks Roxane to read Christian's last letter and Cyrano recites it. Roxane realizes she loved Cyrano all these years and not Christian.

Falling Action – Cyrano dies.

Denouement – Roxane mourns the death of her true love.

How Would You Present the Constructed Movie Framework

Using the plot of discovery and giving it a working title of *Wanderlust: The Beauty of Discovery*, let's do a quick hypothetical example of the narrative structure.

For the plot of discovery, the story could begin with Jack graduating from college (exposition).

Jack is lost after graduation because his whole life has been planned up to this point by his family (conflict).

Jack decides there has to be a better life somewhere, so he leaves and wanders aimlessly to find this new life that he will be able to tolerate (rising action).

At this point, you have a period of rising action, which will tie the conflict/complication to the climax. First, though, there is a lot of moving forward and setbacks to progress through toward the climax, which is the ultimate decision and piece of action for the discovery.

In the mid-West, Jack stops at a rest area on the expressway. A girl about his age asks for a ride to the next state. This is the first rung of the rising action.

Jack does not trust her. Once they get to the next state, he drops her off at the first restaurant he sees, telling her to have a nice life.

Jack continues on but thinks that he should stop and get a job in a town that he has an interest in as he is driving through it. This is the second rung in the rising action ladder.

He finds a job in an office, which he thinks he may like for a short while until it becomes routine.

Jack's job blossoms as the owners want to begin an export operation, and they ask Jack to run it. After long hours of development of the export operation, Jack realizes that he can establish a successful life of his own without parental interference (further rising action movement).

However, the rising action hits a snag (first setback) as Jack nears the official opening of the export operation. The girl he gave a ride to earlier in the movie shows up in this town.

Jack states that maybe he should leave (setback solution to the development that is near the climax).

Climax – Jack continues working on the export operation, but he cannot get his mind off of Betty. He finally realizes he needs someone like Betty, along with a business he established on his own, to create the life he desires. Betty sees him and begins to run away. He catches up to her and kisses her, telling her he made a mistake. He needs her.

During the falling action, Jack finds out that Betty is the owner's daughter. This scene makes for a quick resolution and a movie ending for *Wanderlust: The Beauty of Discovery*.

At this point, a good exercise is to develop a narrative structure for a movie with the plot of revenge. Use the hypothetical example characters, Jack and Suzie, to do this.

Summary of Narrative Structure

Outside of the characters, the narrative structure is the movie. Narrative structure is not only the framework of how a movie is told; it provides an avenue for the characters to grow. The narrative structure consists of the plot and story being portrayed in chronological (linear) order or in a combination of flashbacks and present time (nonlinear).

Narrative structure is a vicious cycle that begins with the plot telling the story how it is going to be told. The story goes through various changes from the exposition to the complication or conflict. As the protagonist or main character progresses through trying to resolve the complication, the protagonist moves the story along so we have rising action. The rising action comes to a climax where the protagonist has to make the ultimate decision of how to handle a situation to push it toward the end. After the climax, comes the falling action, because the main incident just occurred.

At the end of the falling action, the viewer has arrived at the resolution/denouement, ending the movie.

We have established ten different plots plus the plot of inner conflict. Now that the framework for the movie has been constructed, we will discuss what goes over the framework to bring out the style and beauty of the movie—the characters.

Further Viewing

With the completion of this chapter, movies to watch that that are excellent examples of narrative structure are:

- *Citizen Kane*, 1941, directed by Orson Welles, starring Joseph Cotton, Orson Welles, and Agnes Morehead. The narrative structure is nonlinear as it starts with the protagonist's death, and the viewer sees the life of the protagonist through flashbacks.
- *Double Indemnity*, 1944, directed by Billy Wilder, starring Fred MacMurray, Barbara Stanwyck, and Edward G. Robinson. This movie also has a nonlinear narrative structure starting with the wounded protagonist telling how he got shot.
- *The Big Country*, 1958, directed by William Wyler, starring Gregory Peck, Jean Simmons, Carroll Baker, and Charlton Heston. The narrative structure is linear. As the movie moves forward chronologically, the viewer witnesses the thought processes and actions of the main characters as they change.
- *Sophie's Choice*, 1982, directed by Alan J. Pakula, starring Meryl Streep, Kevin Kline, and Peter MacNicol. The narrative structure starts linear as the writer narrates his story. But the movie, in the second half, becomes nonlinear as Sophie tells of her past experiences.
- *The Hurt Locker*, 2008, directed by Kathryn Bigelow, starring Jeremy Renner, Anthony Mackie, and Brian Geraghty. This movie has a linear narrative structure, showing how the protagonist begins to change after each action sequence.

Assignment

Exposition: Alec hires Jack to find his wife Betty. Jack states that Alec's wife will show up. But Alec is nervous about her well-being. Jack agrees to take the case.

Complication: When Jack finds Alec's wife fairly quickly, he decides to do surveillance on her to make sure he has not missed anything during the hiring process. Jack watches her as she goes to her house and then goes shopping. She buys unusual items that clearly have no purpose for a rich housewife. Jack believes whatever Betty does is none of his business as long as she is not in any danger. After watching her for a while, Jack determines everything is all right, gives up on the case and returns home.

Jack's wife, Suzie, tries to convince Jack that he should not have given up the case because something is going to happen to Betty. Jack tries to ignore her, but she keeps after him to continue the surveillance. Jack tells her he has to find new work to make money. After hearing that, Suzie stops nagging. Later, the telephone rings and Suzie answers it. The caller is Betty.

The above are two pieces of the framework for the story. What could the rising action be? What type of plot would it be?

24 "InPoint," http://www.thecinematheque.ca/inpoint/index.html.

25 "Plot," Merriam-Webster Dictionary, http://www.merriam-webster.com/dictionary/plot.

26 "The "Basic" Plots in Literature." Special Collections Created by Ipl2. October 13, 2010. Accessed September 16, 2016. http://www.ipl.org/div/farq/plotFARQ.html.

27 "The "Basic" Plots in Literature." Special Collections Created by Ipl2. October 13, 2010. Accessed September 16, 2016. http://www.ipl.org/div/farq/plotFARQ.html.

28 Ibid.

29 "Story," Merriam-Webster Dictionary, http://www.merriam-webster.com/dictionary/story.

4. How Are the Characters Portrayed?

Dictionary.com defines character as "the aggregate of features and traits that form the individual nature of some person or thing, including moral or ethical quality, reputation, and the qualities of honesty, courage, or the like; integrity."[30]

The portrayal of a character in a movie can also be phrased by the formula: **D**ialogue + **P**hysical **M**ovement = Character.

This leads us to the main ingredient of a movie and why we watch movies: the characters. Identifying with the characters is a common reason people love a certain movie. The viewer wants to see the main character (protagonist) and the supporting characters develop like people do in real life.

In order for the movie to express this development, the character has to show growth in moral and ethical qualities, such as integrity, honesty, or courage, and by having a well-developed background, making the character three-dimensional.

In order to create a three-dimensional character with a well-developed background, the movie has to illustrate the character's sociology, psychology, and physiology. Since a movie is a visual experience, the sociology and psychology, along with the physiology, are subtly portrayed visually by the physical movements and the dialogue the character displays in any particular situation. Physiology is included in this portrayal because many movie characters are self-conscious of their physical appearances, like Cyrano de Bergerac who was self-conscious of his nose.

The physical actions and the dialogue of the character change from the exposition and conflict as he or she goes through the rising and falling action of the movie. Every shot or frame of a film has to count in order to accomplish the action and progress the story. In addition, the dialogue in these situations has to agree with the physical movements. For instance, the dialogue cannot be a ranting and raving of a particular situation while the character is standing calmly, looking out a window.

Let's draw upon the characters from *Detour*, *Cyrano de Bergerac*, and the hypothetical example, *Wanderlust: The Beauty of Discovery*, to see how character is or could be expressed. These examples will provide a good analysis of a character. What the character's mannerisms, movements, and dialogue are reveals aspects of the individual's personality and background and what actions will occur regarding the handling of the movie's conflict.

Character Physiology

The main physiology points of a character are the sex, age, height, weight, posture, appearance, defects, and heredity. A character's voice should also be part of the physiology because different parts of a person's anatomy, such as vocal folds (cords), throat, mouth cavity, nasal passages, the tongue, soft palate, and lips,[31] create sound.

In *Cyrano de Bergerac*, the most prominent physiological characteristic is, obviously, Cyrano's nose. His nose affects both his physical and verbal actions. Would Cyrano de Bergerac have been involved in so many sword fights if his nose was of normal size? Considering his attitude, he might have, but overall probably not. Other characters in the movie that did not have such a pronounced nose were not involved in as many altercations as Cyrano.

Besides sword fighting, he is egotistical in the areas of writing and acting, which compensate for his large nose. The size of his nose affects his actions in life such as his love toward Roxane. Instead

Regarding a character's physiology, the most important and influential part of the movie, Cyrano de Bergerac, is based on Cyrano's nose.

of expressing his love for Roxane near the beginning of the movie, he lives vicariously through Christian.

In *Detour*, actions that occur to Al Roberts slowly wear his body down to the point that exhaustion is evident in his physiology. Being a nightclub singer, Al's voice has to sound pleasing.

The look of a character's physiology, such as a close-up of a character's face, lends toward the mood or atmosphere of a scene. Seeing his dirty, unshaven face and furrowed forehead, the viewer can see the worry in Al Roberts' demeanor.

In the hypothetical example, *Wanderlust: The Beauty of Discovery*, since it is not an actual movie, how would Jack physically appear? From the above list, you can see some of the obvious physiological characteristics for Jack. He is a young male, since he just graduated from college. Throughout the movie, he does not age much as the movie takes place within several months or a year at the most. Most of the other areas, such as voice, height, weight, posture, appearance, defects, and heredity, do not play a significant role for the character Jack, like Cyrano's nose. The rest of his physiology can be nondescript.

Character Psychology

The main psychological points of a character are moral standards, personal premise, ambition, frustrations, chief disappointments, temperament, attitude toward life, complexes, extroversion, introversion; ambivalence, abilities, character qualities, and IQ. These psychological points form the background of a character and determine logically how he or she is going to act at the beginning of the movie, during the rising action of the conflict, and in the final action at the climax of the movie. Even though some of the psychological traits are not shown at the beginning of the movie, these traits are brought out by the conflict that arises and the situations that occur during the rising action of the movie.

In *Cyrano de Bergerac*, Cyrano is frustrated by his belief that he is not desirable to Roxane because of his nose. This frustration is fueled throughout the movie, and it results in a temperament whereby he ridicules other people, such as he did the actor at the beginning of the movie. Cyrano's chief disappointment is that he never tells Roxane he loves her.

Cyrano is an ambivert. He is an extrovert to everyone except for Roxane. To Roxane, he is an introvert, because he keeps everything inside and does not pronounce his true love to her.

In *Detour*, Al Roberts' attitude toward life at the beginning of the movie is that he is satisfied playing piano in a nightclub and marrying Sue, the singer in the nightclub. Al's attitude toward life changes after he accidentally kills two people. He is frustrated and quick tempered by these two deaths, resulting in a changed attitude toward life.

In *Wanderlust: The Beauty of Discovery*, Jack has ambition as he wants to develop a career on his own. This becomes Jack's main attitude toward life. At the beginning of the movie, though, he has a temperament of frustration, because his family has planned his whole life up to the point of his graduation from college. What else would you add to the psychology of Jack?

Character Sociology

The main sociological points of a character are economic class, occupation, education, home life, religion, race, nationality, position in the community, political affiliation, amusements, and hobbies. Depending upon the story of the movie, the sociology may not play as big a part in the character portrayal as the psychology of the character. If a character is taken out, away from the way of living that he or she has adapted to and is familiar with, sociology may play a bigger part in the movie.

In *Cyrano de Bergerac*, Cyrano is an accomplished swordsman and poet. He has an education and a favorable place in the community. His name is well-known.

In *Detour*, Al Roberts is a working class individual who is employed as a piano player. He is a middle-class individual with no home life. His religion, race, and nationality are immaterial to his situation.

In *Wanderlust: The Beauty of Discovery*, Jack has a sociological background with a specific economic class and home life that is symbolic of the well-to-do middle class. His family is a respected part of the community. Jack wants to change all that by searching for a future away from his family and home town. Social adjustment is going to be the biggest adaption that he has to go through in the movie.

Analysis of the Three-Dimensional Characters

Each of the three characters has a specific physiology, psychology, and sociology. These attributes are stronger in one of the three areas than the others. The one strong attribute helps to progress the story by showing how the protagonist deals with the conflict.

Cyrano de Bergerac's primary character dimension is physiology. How he deals with his physiology affects his psychological actions of love toward Roxane. This presents the conflict and rising action, including the forward progressions and the setbacks, in the movie.

Al Roberts' primary character dimension is psychology. His temperament changes throughout the movie because of the accidental deaths that have occurred. These deaths contributed to a developing temperament of hostility and helplessness, resulting in a fatalistic demeanor.

Jack's primary character dimension is sociology. He has built a whole life based on his family's place in the community and his education. Now he wants to reinvent himself by moving away and establishing a new sociological background. The idea of reinventing himself drives his actions. He becomes egotistical in the process because he is looking out for himself and what he wants to do rather than assisting anyone else. No matter if he likes it or not, he has become a product of his controlling family.

Visually Demonstrating the Three-Dimensional Character

We have looked at the physical and mental backgrounds of three different characters based on their physiology, psychology, and sociology. How are these characters brought to life on the screen where everything is visually expressed? Before the cameras role and the film is edited, what is done?

Mise-en-scene is defined as all of the elements or visual elements that are in a shot. These elements are setting, lighting, staging, costumes, and make-up. The set refers to furniture and props and everything that dresses the set or is contained in the décor of the set. Staging refers to the blocking and physical action of a character.

Previously, we saw photos of Al Roberts from *Detour* and Cyrano from *Cyrano de Bergerac*. Make-up was used to express their physiological traits, such as Cyrano's nose. It was also used to demonstrate what the character had been going through, such as the dirt on Al Roberts' face.

At the beginning of the movie, you get to know something about the character and the time period. In the beginning of *Cyrano de Bergerac*, the viewer sees the costume that Cyrano had on, along with what the interior setting of a theatre was like during the seventeenth century.

The interior setting at the beginning of *Detour* is a diner. The diner is small and confining, like Al's life, and he believes the police will eventually capture him. The diner is staged with the type of people, like truck drivers, who frequent that sort of restaurant when on the road travelling.

We will take a more in-depth follow-up look at mise-en-scene in the production chapters of directing (Chapter Five), cinematography (Chapter Six), and editing (Chapter Seven) to see how mise-en-scene is used by these areas of production to express a character and to further the story.

The Three-Dimensional Character Demonstrated Through Sound

Different aspects of sound enhance the character and story, making the movie a complete experience. Sound in a movie includes dialogue, music, sound effects, ambient noise, or background noise and soundtracks. Sound has always been around—even for silent movies. During the silent movie period, musical accompaniment was provided in theatres.

In the late 1920s movies began to "talk." Many students have indicated in the film courses that I have taught that sound was the biggest innovation to movies. Dialogue is a conversation between at least two characters in a movie to exchange ideas and resolve a problem.

Dialogue is an important aspect of the sound in the movie. Even during the silent movie period there was dialogue. However, the dialogue was written on silent movie dialogue cards.

Music, whether referring to the musical score at the beginning and end of the movie, along with background music to set the tone and atmosphere of a scene, assist in leading the viewer through a complete movie experience. The music may also be symbolic of the personality of the character and the action he or she is going through at any particular time in the movie.

Sound effects, according to dictionary.com, are any sound, other than music or speech, artificially reproduced to create an effect in a dramatic presentation, such as the sound of a storm or a creaking door. These sounds heighten the action of the movie, and it heightens the interest in the characters to see what will happen to them next.

Ambient noises provide realism to a scene, giving naturalism to the area that the character is in during a particular time of the movie.

Soundtracks are musical accompaniment for a movie, such as a popular song or songs and music from the movie. The soundtrack could have a song expressing the background or a specific characteristic of the character. The soundtrack could also have music that is expressive of the story.

With the different aspects of sound expressing different features of the characters and the situation the characters are in, sound progresses the story and plot.

We will take a more in-depth follow-up look at sound in the production chapters of directing (Chapter Five), editing (Chapter Seven), and sound (Chapter Eight) to see how sound is used by these areas of production to enhance the character and progress the story of the movie.

Further Character Dissection

This brief discussion of the character outlines the complexity in building and developing a character in a movie that is going to last on an average of 120 minutes.

As we have read in previous chapters, a lot of action occurs in a movie, and the characters have to stay consistent with the construction of the movie. This is why the exposition is a very delicate part, but an extremely important part, of the story, because the main characters and their backgrounds have to be introduced. But the introduction cannot take too long because the audience will lose interest in the movie.

Enough of the main characters' personalities have to be portrayed during the exposition so the rest of the movie has a logical progression as the audience gets to learn more and more about the characters. And, as the audience gets more and more involved with the characters and their story, the audience becomes more wrapped up in the movie resulting in an enjoyable experience for them.

Remember—with the theme, the purpose of the movie has been established. With the establishing of the purpose of the movie, the question has to be asked, "What is the best way to demonstrate the purpose of the movie?" Do the characters demonstrate this purpose?

The next question is: Do the characters work well together? Are the characters friends, enemies, or do they work together? Is this a good combination to form a good relationship and an interesting movie?

The last question is: Is the story different enough that the characters and their actions weave an interesting tapestry to make movie viewers interested in them for at least 90 minutes? This is a difficult question to answer but one that is left up to the viewer's preference. In this contemporary period, are the potential actions of the characters and the weaving of the story interesting enough in these movies? Did the movie follow the format in an interesting manner?

After taking a beginning look and discussing the characters, what stands out as being the most important: story, plot, narrative structure, setting, or characters? What stands out as being the most memorable? What do you go to the movies for? Are you interested enough in the characters that you want to see what happens to them?

If your response is "yes" to the above questions, then you were already hooked from the beginning of the movie. If you are interested in seeing what happens to the characters that is a positive sign too. If you are ready to leave the movie theatre, then the movie is not for you.

As previously outlined in an earlier chapter, the movie action between the conflict and the climax is referred to as rising action. The action between the climax and the resolution is the falling action. Rising action is not always rising. It is more of an up-and-down motion, because the main characters have setbacks and have to start over.

Summary of Character Portrayal

Characters are the essence of a movie. Good characters are three-dimensional based on the character's physiology, psychology, and sociology. One of the three areas may often be predominant over the others and is affected more by the story, but all have to be developed to give depth to the character.

The characters have to work well together to keep the audience interested, along with dialogue worth listening to and action worth watching. The story helps a great deal with bringing this to fruition, allowing the characters to interact with one another, and to develop logically to the climax and resolution of the movie. In this way, the audience gets caught up in the movie and wants to watch more. A good movie is like a good book; the characters have to be very satisfying. But unlike a book, a movie is a visual and audio experience. The character development has to be shown and heard.

Further Viewing

These movies are excellent examples of character portrayal:

- *Mrs. Miniver*, 1942, directed by William Wyler, starring Greer Garson, Walter Pigeon, and Teresa Wright. The three stars portray people in England at the beginning of World War II and the struggles they persevered.
- *The Best Years of Our Lives*, 1946, directed by William Wyler, starring Frederic March, Dana Andrews, and Harold Russell. This movie follows the efforts to adjust to civilian life for a soldier, airman, and sailor after World War II.
- *Ben-Hur*, 1959, directed by William Wyler, starring Charlton Heston, Jack Hawkins, and Stephen Boyd. The main character, Judah Ben-Hur, is falsely convicted and sentenced to be a galley slave. Once freed, he seeks revenge. This is a movie of character growth and change.
- *Elmer Gantry*, 1960, directed by Richard Brooks, starring Burt Lancaster, Jean Simmons, and Arthur Kennedy. This movie follows fast-talking salesman, Elmer Gantry, and his experiences with revivalism and a female lay preacher.
- *To Kill a Mockingbird*, 1962, directed by Robert Mulligan, starring Gregory Peck, Frank Overton, and William Windom. This movie follows a lawyer in the Depression-Era South who defends a black man accused of raping a white girl.

Assignment

As Jack is finishing an undercover investigation case, he comes to realize, as he looks around his small motel room, that he is successful in another dead-end job and has no friends. He cannot have any friends, especially girlfriends, because he cannot bring them back to his place, because they may find out that he is an undercover investigator. Jack contemplates another career. His decision is to go back to college to major in his only interest, theatre. He quits his job and enrolls in college for the spring semester. Jack finds out he only has to go for one semester and take courses in his major. Upon hearing this, Jack believes his luck is changing.

On the first day of class, Jack is apprehensive because he does not know what to expect, and everybody will be younger than he. When he enters the class, which is in a theatre, he sees that it is worse than he expected, because everybody knows one another except for him. When class begins, though, all is forgotten when he listens to the professor, Alec Morgan. Jack is excited because he has Prof. Morgan for most of his classes. Jack heard that Alec had won a Tony Award, which initially interested him in enrolling in the college.

Hearing Alec speak about theatre, Jack becomes more interested in theatre, and wants to develop his talent to become successful in theatre. Jack has a tough schedule, as he obtained a job in the security department at the college working the midnight shift. Jack works all night, goes home, and changes for his 9:00 am class.

Do a character analysis of Jack based on the above information to make him a three-dimensional character.

30 "Character," Dictionary.com, http://www.dictionary.com/browse/character?s=t.

31 The Voice Foundation, http://voicefoundation.org/about/what-is-tvf/.

Part II: Production

Prologue

In this section, since we are dealing with actual professions, we are going to take a different approach. Now that you know the different building blocks of a movie, you may wonder how to put them all together.

We are going to take a look at different production areas by putting you in those positions. You are the director; you are the director and cinematographer; you are the director and editor; and you are the director and sound technician.

We will go through different terminology for each of the areas. Then we will take a look at how they apply in different examples of the three movies you watched and with a hypothetical example. The more knowledge you have, the better appreciation and the better decisions you can make in situations given in the assignments.

5. What Is Directing?

Dictionary.com defines directing as "to manage or guide by advice, helpful information, instruction, etc."[32] However, this is a general definition of directing. How can we make it more specific for a movie director?

The portrayal of the director can be phrased by the formula: **C**inematography + **S**etting + **B**locking + **A**cting + **E**diting = **D**irecting.

In other words, the director is the chief creative person for a movie. The director leads the viewer so the viewer gets the most out of the movie. The director wants the viewer to see the story from a particular point of view.

Like a stage director, a movie director tells the actors how to play a particular scene, sets the scene for a specific type of mood, and moves the actors around for a particular effect. In the above definition, the word setting is referring to the specific atmosphere created by the props, location, scenery, and costumes.

The directing of cinematography includes both the camera shots and the lighting to obtain both a particular type of effect and mood. The director also has control over the editing to create the pace, rhythm, coherence, story, and character development they and the producer want.

Finally, most directors are involved with the sound for the movie, especially the dialogue, ambient noises, and sound effects. Many directors have their individual style, so we can often recognize when a specific director is responsible for a movie. This is referred to as auteur theory.

However, in this chapter, we are going to concentrate on the main visual and verbal direction of the setting, lighting, blocking, costumes, and dialogue and how they contribute to the story, character development and character portrayal of the movie. We will analyze the different viewpoints so you will see and judge for yourself if the actions taken were the best direction, cinematography, sound, and editing for these movies.

We will touch upon the cinematography, editing, and sound as it pertains to the director's emphasis of the aforementioned areas in the story, character development, and the character portrayal. We will go into more in-depth detail of the cinematography, editing, and sound in Chapter Six, "What Is Cinematography?"; Chapter Seven, "What Is Editing?"; and Chapter Eight, "What is Sound?"

Let's look at the setting, lighting, blocking, costumes, characters, and dialogue and how they are expressed by the director in the cinematography, sound, and editing.

Mise-en-scene, as discussed in Chapter Four, encompasses the setting, lighting, actors' blocking, and costumes. The setting includes both the location, such as an apartment, and the props. Mise-en-scene is everything that is contained in a cinematographic shot.

This is a big task. Normally, the director is assisted by the production designer for the setting, the costume designer for the costumes, and the cinematographers for the lighting. Each of the designers and cinematographers has a staff that they work with.

Mise-en-scene is a good technique to use for the exposition of the story.

Without speaking a word, a director can express the mindset of the protagonist with a single shot of his or her apartment. Is the apartment messy or neat? How is the character dressed, and what type of movement is the protagonist making? If the movement is rapid, is the character in a hurry? How does the character look? Are the movements lackadaisical? What is the protagonist wearing? Are the clothes old and dirty? Are the clothes neat and clean? How is the lighting in the apartment? Is the lighting bright, shadowy, or dark with no interior lights turned on?

Without the character saying a word, and with only a short burst of the camera, all the above questions can be answered.

Remember the hypothetical example of Jack in *Wanderlust: The Beauty of Discovery*? As the director, how would you like the audience initially to view him? Jack is graduating from college, and he still lives at home with his parents. What would his parents' house be like? How would Jack's bedroom appear? Do you want him to be sloppy, with a messy room, or neat and organized, to match the rest of the house? Do a college graduate's accommodations have to match his mind, which is probably organized, to be able to graduate from college?

What would the dialogue of a character sound like when he or she is in a conversation? The tone and what is said is very important in determining the type of person the protagonist is. A combination of both the visual and the audio are very good in displaying the character portrayal. The tone and language, combined with the physical and facial expressions, are very good in determining the background of the character and the actions the character may take regarding the conflict.

How would Jack's conversation go with Betty? Jack has a one-track mind. He wants to make something of himself without any help from his parents. Jack does not want any distractions, which Betty is. Jack's dialogue with her would be to the point. He does not want to get to know her because this would jeopardize his chance of establishing the type of career that he desires.

Now, let's look at how all of the above information is expressed for each of the three movies and for their genres.

Directing Points of the Comedy Viewed

How would you, as the director, express the story and characters in *The Front Page*? How do your ideas compare to the director, Lewis Milestone?

An Internet Movie Data Base (IMDb) biography of Lewis Milestone states that Milestone's movies are noted for his taut editing, snappy dialogue, and clever visual touches.[33] He is a good example of a director that touches on the areas of cinematography, editing, and sound. Snappy, rapid dialogue was often a signature feature of the comedies of the 1930s and 1940s. There were many instances of the snappy dialogue in the press room in *The Front Page*.

The quick, rapid dialogue is a very important part of the movie. The dialogue shows that newspaper reporters can very quickly throw questions at someone in order to get the information they need.

When Hildy Johnson hides Earl Williams in the desk, he shows how quickly he can come up with a plan. This action also shows that Hildy is not completely honest. Rather than turning Earl Williams over to the police, like an honest person would, he hides Earl Williams in the desk.

Visually, in movies, actions can say more for a character than words. Molly Malloy, a supporting character in the movie, is an acquaintance of Earl Williams. She jumps out the press room window to distract the reporters, so that they do not discover Earl Williams in the desk. Ignoring any dialogue prior to jumping, what does the act of jumping signify about her personality?

The actions of Walter Burns both progress the action of the story and demonstrate his character and Hildy's character. Walter pulls a fire alarm, and Hildy runs to the street to see what was going on. This blocking shows that Walter is a conniving individual, and the viewer can see, from almost the beginning of the movie, that Hildy does not want to quit the newspaper. What Hildy states and does are two different behaviors.

Directing Points of the Crime Drama Viewed

How would you, as the director, express the story and characters in *Detour*? How do you think your ideas compare to the director, Edgar G. Ulmer? Do you think that the negative outcomes of each action make Al Roberts an unlucky individual?

The physical movements and facial expressions of Charles Haskell and Vera coincide very well with the dialogue in those scenes. The accidental death of both of these characters progresses the story and illustrates the future for Al. The shadows and the night, along with the cramped setting of the diner, express the life style that has become Al's.

Directing Points of the Historical Drama Viewed

How would you, as the director express the story and characters in *Cyrano de Bergerac*? How do your ideas compare to the director, Michael Gordon?

The visual action is very important and the mise-en-scene is developed to show the type of places that Cyrano frequents, such as the theatre. This demonstrates that he is a learned man. The amount of sword fighting he is involved with indicates he is a talented swordsman. However, his hiding when he is feeding the romantic language to Christian points to his conflicted personality. He is confident in certain situations when his physiology does not matter to him. When the love of someone does matter to him, he hides because he is afraid of what the truth might bring.

Language and dialogue are very important in this movie, especially toward the end when Christian is dead. The language and dialogue are important because of what is said but because of what is not said. For 14 years Cyrano never stated that he wrote the words that Christian stated. Cyrano only tells Roxane before he dies of a mortal wound. Does Cyrano write the satirical essays to purposefully get killed so he does not have to face Roxane, the woman he has always loved?

Final Thoughts on Directing

The director shapes the story, or the script, so a particular emphasis is stressed and a specific theme or discourse is presented. A particular point is put forth. The director decides on or contributes to the cinematography, the sound, and the editing of the scenes for a movie. In so doing, the director shapes the movement and dialogue of the actors, along with their character portrayal. The director is also responsible for the prop placement, the costumes, and the location of the different shots.

Did you see the development that was taking place for each of the genres? What was different in the development of each of the movie genres? As an armchair director, what would you change about these three aforementioned movies? What would you emphasize differently? Always keep in mind that the producer has the final word.

We will travel on to the final three chapters and go into the cinematography, the editing and the sound in more detail to give a clearer exemplified overview of these three moviemaking areas.

Further Viewing

With the completion of this chapter, further movies to watch that are excellent examples of directing are:

- *Lawrence of Arabia*, 1962, directed by David Lean, starring Peter O'Toole, Alec Guinness, and Anthony Quinn. This movie is an excellent example in cinematography and character development.

- *The Godfather*, 1972, directed by Francis Ford Coppola, starring Marlon Brando, Al Pacino, and James Caan. This movie is an excellent example of timelessness, presenting a topic that is still pertinent over four decades later.
- *Breaker Morant*, 1980, directed by Bruce Beresford, starring Edward Woodward, Jack Thompson, and Bryon Brown. This movie is an excellent example of timelessness, presenting a topic that is still pertinent over three decades later.
- *Schindler's List*, 1993, directed by Steven Spielberg, starring Liam Neeson, Ralph Fiennes, and Ben Kingsley. This movie is an excellent example in directing a realistic view of a dark chapter in the history of the world.
- *Pulp Fiction*, 1994, directed by Quentin Tarantino, starring John Travolta, Uma Thurman, and Samuel L. Jackson. This movie is an excellent example of a different directing style of storytelling.

Assignment

As Jack looks at Alec, he has a flashback to when they first met. Jack enters the bar that they are in, and Suzie asks Jack to buy her some flowers because it is her birthday. Jack buys the flowers for Suzie. Alec walks over to Jack and states that he should not buy her anything else or she may want to move in and live with him. Jack states that would be tough because he is a poor college student and does not have a place. Suzie states that college students are not poor. Alec tells Jack that he has been there for a while and has heard every line. Jack asks Alec why he is in Latin America. Alec states that he got discharged from the service and he did not want to return to the United States. Jack asks why, and Alec states that he wanted to try not being under the weight of the rules, policies, and authority of the United States. Jack asks Alec when he is going to return to the United States. Alec states, "When life is better in the United States."

Back to the present, sitting at the table, Alec asks Jack if the doctor told him everything. Jack states as far as he knows, yes. Alec says that he told the doctor to tell Jack everything. Jack asks if Alec wants to return to the United States to his parents' home. Alec states that he does not. Alec states that his existence now is just fine. Suzie asks them what is going on. Alec tells her that in six months, at the most, the trio will be a duo.

As the movie director, how would you direct the scenes above regarding mise-en-scene, cinematography, editing, and sound?

32 "Directing," Dictionary.com, http://www.dictionary.com/browse/directing?s=t.

33 "Lewis Milestone," IMDb, http://www.imdb.com/name/nm0587277/.

6. What Is Cinematography?

Dictionary.com defines cinematography as "the art or technique of motion-picture photography."[34] Being a technical area, we do not want to put a simple formula in place.

The director, being the chief creative person for a movie, is in charge of the cinematography with the director of photography or the cinematographer being in charge of the actual camera, lighting, and electrical crews.

Wikibooks, in their "Movie Making Manual," defines the director of photography (DP) as being "in charge of the actual image of a film project. They direct the camera/grip/lighting crews as to how the lights should be placed, how the camera should be exposed, and basically anything related to the film image. They will also choose the film stock and processing for the film. Many times the DP will be present during color timing as well. The DP works very closely with the Director to realize his vision of how the film should look."[35]

The quickest way to view different camera shots and how they are used is by watching the following YouTube video.

Cinematography Lesson One: Angles by Nathan Grebe

https://youtu.be/nHCpVgkpleQ

Vocabulary

Extremely wide shot: Shows a broad view of the surroundings of the character and informs the audience as to what is going on. It is often used as an opening shot to a new scene.

Wide shot: Shows the character from head to toe.

Medium wide shot: Shows the character, usually cut off below the knees, but it is wide enough to show the settings around him or her and still be close enough to show the expressions on his or her face.

Medium shot: Shows the upper body, arms, and head.

Close up: Face and shoulders are showing, and it shows the expression on the character's face very well.

Extreme close up: Only part of a character's face is visible. It fills up the entire frame with details.

Angles:

> High Angle: The camera, placed above eye level, is looking downward. This shot is often used to make the character seem small, weak, young, or confused.

> Medium Angle: Most commonly used.

> Low Angle: Used to make the character seem bigger, stronger, more frightening, or nobler.

Over the shoulder: Close up of the character shown over the shoulder of another character.

Two shot: Both characters are shown in the frame. The camera moves.

Pan: The camera rotates side to side, while remaining in the same location. It is simply executed with a tripod.

Tilt: The camera is moved to aim upward or downward without changing location. Also done with a tripod.

Zoom: Basically, zoom is moving the lens without moving the camera around. I would not recommend using this feature with a DSLR camera simply because it causes a fair amount of shakiness to your video and will take the audience out of the scene. There are always exceptions, though, if the effect you desire needs a zoom, then use the zoom. If you have a prime/fixed lens, you can use your feet to create a zoom.

Dolly: The camera moves side to side. This movement can be used to reveal something in a scene.

An extreme wide shot, as indicated below, is used at the beginning of a scene when the director wants to identify where the scene is taking place. The establishing shot is a photo of a location that the viewer is familiar with, so immediate recognition of the setting for the scene by the viewer is accomplished.

A wide shot or long shot is used when a group of people are being filmed, as in an action scene.

A medium or mid shot films an individual from the waist up. Medium shots are often used when filming a conversation. When the director wants both people involved in a conversation to be seen at the same time, a two shot is used. If three people are involved in a conversation the director may use a three shot technique. When the director wants only one person in a shot, the person speaking may be shown and then when this person stops speaking the reaction of the other person may be displayed in a separate shot.

The close-up shot is used in an emotional scene. This shot is used for very dramatic scenes where the director wants the audience to feel emotion toward the character in a particular scene.

The two-shot and three-shot films are used when two or three people are in the same framed shot.

A director may wish to use this type of shot when he wants the viewer to watch the person doing the talking and the reaction of the individual or individuals listening at the same time.

The over-the-shoulder shot and the point-of-view shot are used when the director wants to give the audience a subjective viewpoint or make the audience feel like they are part of the action.

The over-the-shoulder shot is taken over the shoulder of one of the characters so the viewer sees the shoulder and one side of the face and neck of the one individual as this person is talking to another individual. The viewer actually sees what the first character is looking at. In other words, this puts the viewer in the shoes of one of the characters, so that the viewer is able to see the reaction of the other character.

The point-of-view shot gives the viewer the exact observation of what a character sees without the shoulder and side of the head in the shot. This shot is more of a first-person view, where the viewer sees exactly what the character is seeing.

The previous camera shots and camera positions are discussed to provide a visual literacy between the viewer, and an image that was created and interpreted by the director and the camera crew as the story progresses and the character portrayals develop and change.

Lighting

Lighting assists in establishing a background to the visual literacy that the director and movie crew are creating. Lighting is done in a three-point process.

- The first point is key lighting that provides essential lighting to the object, person or area that you want to light for a shot.
- The second point is fill lighting. If there is only a little fill lighting, then there are many shadows, and it gives a dark and mysterious appearance. More fill light fills in the dark areas of an image.
- The last point is back lighting and it gives a three-dimensional appearance to an object or person.

The design below includes a fourth point of lighting, that is, background lighting. This is used if there is an object with a specific background that needs to be lit for a special reason.

Low-key light and no-fill light leaves shadows. This is the type of mood that would be appropriate for crime, horror, or film noir movies. The higher the key and fill lighting are; the brighter and happier the mood of the movie or scene is. A lot of key and fill lighting is appropriate for comedies and musicals.

Three to four minutes into the movie, *Detour*, there is a good example of bright key light that becomes darker with shadows, and then the key light gets brighter again as the movie moves to a flashback.

We will move away from the cinematography and go to the editing to assemble the shots in the best way possible. These are the two processes that make a movie different from other productions such as live theatre performances.

Standard Three-Point Lighting

#3 Back Light

Object

#1 Key Light

#2 Fill Light

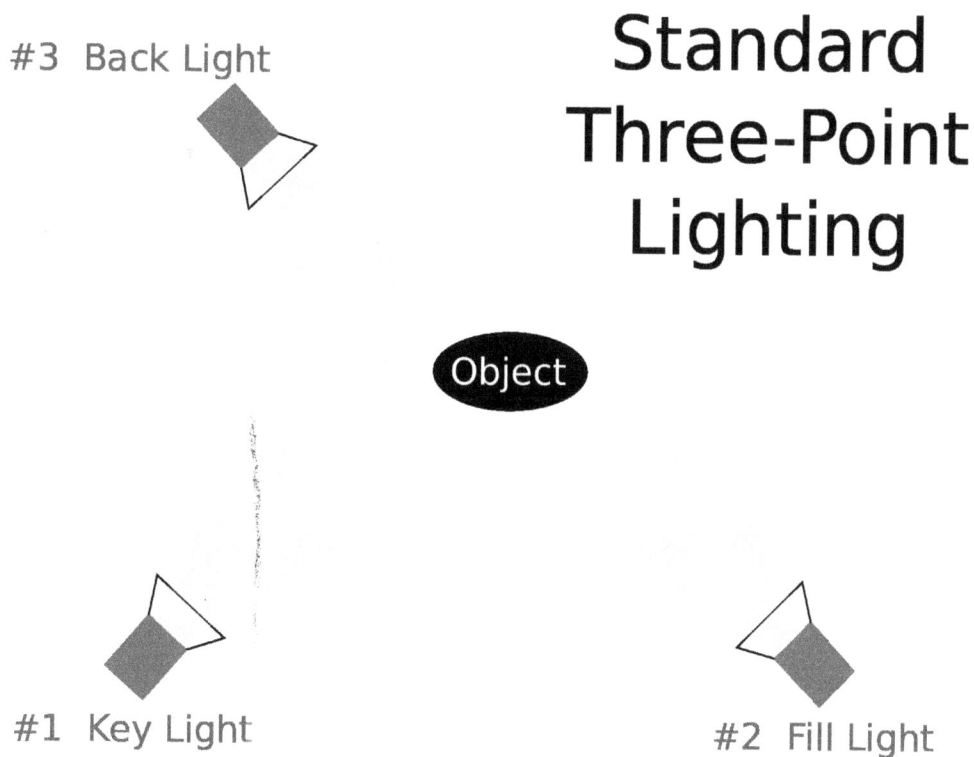

This design is courtesy of the topic, "Three-Point Lighting," from Wikipedia.[36]

Further Viewing

With the completion of this chapter, movies to watch that that are excellent examples of cinematography are:

The 7th Dawn, 1964, directed by Lewis Gilbert, starring William Holden, Susannah York, and Capucine. This movie is an excellent example in scenery cinematography of the Far East.

Chinatown, 1974, directed by Roman Polanski, starring Jack Nicholson, Faye Dunaway, and John Huston. This movie is an excellent example in light and shadows of neo noir.

Days of Heaven, 1978, directed by Terrence Malick, starring Richard Gere, Brooke Adams, and Sam Shepard. This movie is an excellent example of cinematography establishing the turn-of-the-century atmosphere.

Blade Runner, 1982, directed by Ridley Scott, starring Harrison Ford, Rutger Hauer, and Sean Young. This movie is an excellent example in demonstrating futuristic fears.

The Revenant, 2015, directed by Alejandro G. Iñárritu, starring Leonardo DiCaprio, Tom Hardy, and Will Poulter. This movie is an excellent example of realism in action cinematography.

In this scene from the movie, The Front Page, the key light and fill light are high in this shot with Adolph Menjou and Pat O'Brien, which is often the case with comedies.

Assignment

Jack moves into the guest house of Betty and Alec. Betty has hired Jack, a private investigator, to do surveillance on Alec.

Jack is bored and wants to leave a couple of times, but Betty appears and stops him because the situation is getting worse around the house. Betty states that many men she has never seen have come to the house to see Alec. Jack states, "What does that matter?" Alec goes to visit Jack and states that all is not what it looks like, and that Jack is not to believe Betty. Alec states that he has taken precautions because of this.

One night, Alec asks the relatives to come over for a party. Everybody gets drunk and starts running around the yard, kissing the first person they see, regardless of the gender. At one point, Alec is with Betty, and Alec starts to get rough with Betty. Jack cannot see what is going on and what is being said, so he starts to get closer. Suddenly Alec turns around with a surprised look on his face and a gun in his hand. Jack shoots him with Alec still looking mystified by the gun in his hand. The relatives, including Betty, run around hysterically as Jack calls the police. The police arrive, and they find that Alec is dead. They take Jack in to headquarters to go over what happened.

What type of cinematography shots would best express the above scenes?

34 "Cinematography," Dictionary.com, http://www.dictionary.com/browse/cinematography?s=t.

35 "Movie Making Manual/Post-production/Editing," Wikibooks, last modified July 16, 2012, https://en.wikibooks.org/wiki/Movie_Making_Manual/Post-production/Editing.

36 "Three-Point Lighting," Wikipedia, last modified March 22, 2016, https://en.wikipedia.org/wiki/Three-point_lighting.

7. What Is Editing?

Dictionary.com defines edit as "to prepare (motion-picture film, video, or magnetic tape) by deleting, arranging, and splicing, by synchronizing the sound record with the film, etc."[37]

One way to define editing is to use the formula: Shot < Scene < Sequence = Editing.

A shot is defined as a short, continuous single run of the film. A scene is composed of numerous shots cut, and they are joined together. A scene can be anything that the director wants it to be, such as someone entering a room, having a conversation with a person in the room, and then leaving the room. A sequence is a number of scenes joined together that could be a large percentage of the movie when it is finished.

Many terms are used when discussing film editing and how it is done. From the novice viewpoint, we are going to introduce you to the primary areas of film editing so you understand the general process of movie editing. In order to do this, we will go through the editing process, some of the editing techniques and principles, and the cutting transitions that go from one shot to another to develop the different scenes and sequences for a movie.

Editing Process

The producer hires the editor. Editing is performed in the post-production process. Editing is a very labor intensive job in movie making with a certain amount of stress with having to meet a deadline. The editor works closely with the director during different phases of the editing process. The editor has to review the angles of all of the different cameras used for a particular shot to edit the best shots together for the scene. This makes an extra task in the editing organizational process—besides arranging all the different angle shots together.

The movie editing process goes through stages, similar to writing a college term paper. Writing a college term paper consists of getting an idea, writing the rough draft, doing a revision, and then creating the final version. *Wikibooks* states that an editor, too, goes through four stages: logging and assembly, the first rough cut, the main edit, and the fine cut.[38] This editing process is only an example of the procedure because every movie editor, like anyone, has his or her own procedure or routine that he or she follows.

The logging and assembly process is becoming familiar with all of the shots in the movie. The editor watches and listens to all of the material. In a notebook, the editor makes a log of his or her reactions to all of the shots and writes down any ideas that pop into his or her head. The editor uses a time code to link thoughts to specific shots. For a long project, the first edit would be a simple version consisting of all of the wide shots strung together. This assembly would contain the fewest number of edits required to tell the story. The assembly edit allows the editor to get a sense of the project, as a whole, before specifics are focused on.

With the first rough cut, the editor takes one scene at a time and works through all of the takes to find the best, most-consistent material. The scenes may be cut in any order with the point to let each scene work on its own. When the editor has a good working version of a scene, it will be placed into the assembly so the cut gradually builds in complexity. The editor continues to keep a record of all choices made. The rough cut keeps the sound synced together with its picture. The editor should begin to mute or delete unneeded audio, but additional sounds are not added at this point. The first rough cut is completed when each scene has been looked at individually, and it is placed into the edit. The editor should take a break to view the cut without stopping, taking notes of changes that he or she would like to try.

The main edit begins the process of approaching a fine cut. Scenes will have individual problems, and issues will become interdependent between scenes. Key sound effects and music may be introduced at this stage, and the complexity will grow. The editor continues to save each version. The stage, when a rough cut becomes a fine cut, is not exact, but is often when the editor feels each idea has been fully explored. The editor should bring in others to watch the fine cut.

The fine cut is the process of getting down to perfect frame accuracy for every single edit in the film and making sure that each moment flows as best it can. Once the fine cut is approved, the picture is considered "locked" and no further changes will occur. The project will move into full sound post-production and the editor's work is done.

The editing procedure is like any creative job, such as any type of writing. In writing, the stages of the creative process are to write, re-write, re-write, and re-write. The editing process is view, re-view, re-view, review, and view again. When the shots are edited into scenes, certain terminology is used that refers to what the editor is looking for in the final product, along with terminology that is used when describing the type of edit that was used.

Editing Techniques & Principles

The editor begins with all the film footage. Footage is the raw, unedited material as it was originally filmed by the movie camera or recorded by a video camera, which usually must be edited to create a motion picture, video clip, television show, or similar completed work.[39]

Continuity editing is a system of cutting to maintain a continuous and clear narrative action. Continuity editing relies upon matching screen direction, position, and temporal relations from shot to shot. The film supports the viewer's assumption that space and time are contiguous between successive shots.[40] Logical coherence is achieved through continuity editing.

One technique that is used is a B-Roll. A B-Roll is supplemental or alternative footage intercut with the main shot.[41]

A basic principle in editing is the 180-degree rule. The 180-degree rule[42] is a basic guideline regarding the on-screen spatial relationship between a character and another character or object within a scene. An imaginary line, called the axis, connects the characters, and by keeping the camera on one side of this axis for every shot in the scene, the first character is always frame right of the second character, who is then always frame left of the first. The camera passing over the axis is called jumping the line or crossing the line; breaking the 180-degree rule by shooting on all sides is known as shooting in the round.

The last main area of editing that the director wants to arrive at is the appropriate rhythm for the movie. Yale Film Studies elaborates the concept of movie rhythm by defining it as the "perceived rate and regularity of sounds, series of shots and movements within the shots. Rhythmic factors include beat or pulse, accent or stress and tempo or pace. Rhythm is one of the essential features of a film, for it decisively contributes to its mood and overall impression on the viewer. . . . It is achieved through the combination of mise-en-scene, cinematography, sound and editing. Rhythm can be understood as the final balance of all the elements of a film.[44]

Finally, a montage is a technique in film editing in which a series of short shots are edited into a sequence to condense space, time, and information.[45]

Editing Transitions

A "cut" in editing refers the splicing of two shots together. This cut is made by the film editor at the editing stage of a film. Between sequences, the cut marks a rapid transition between one time

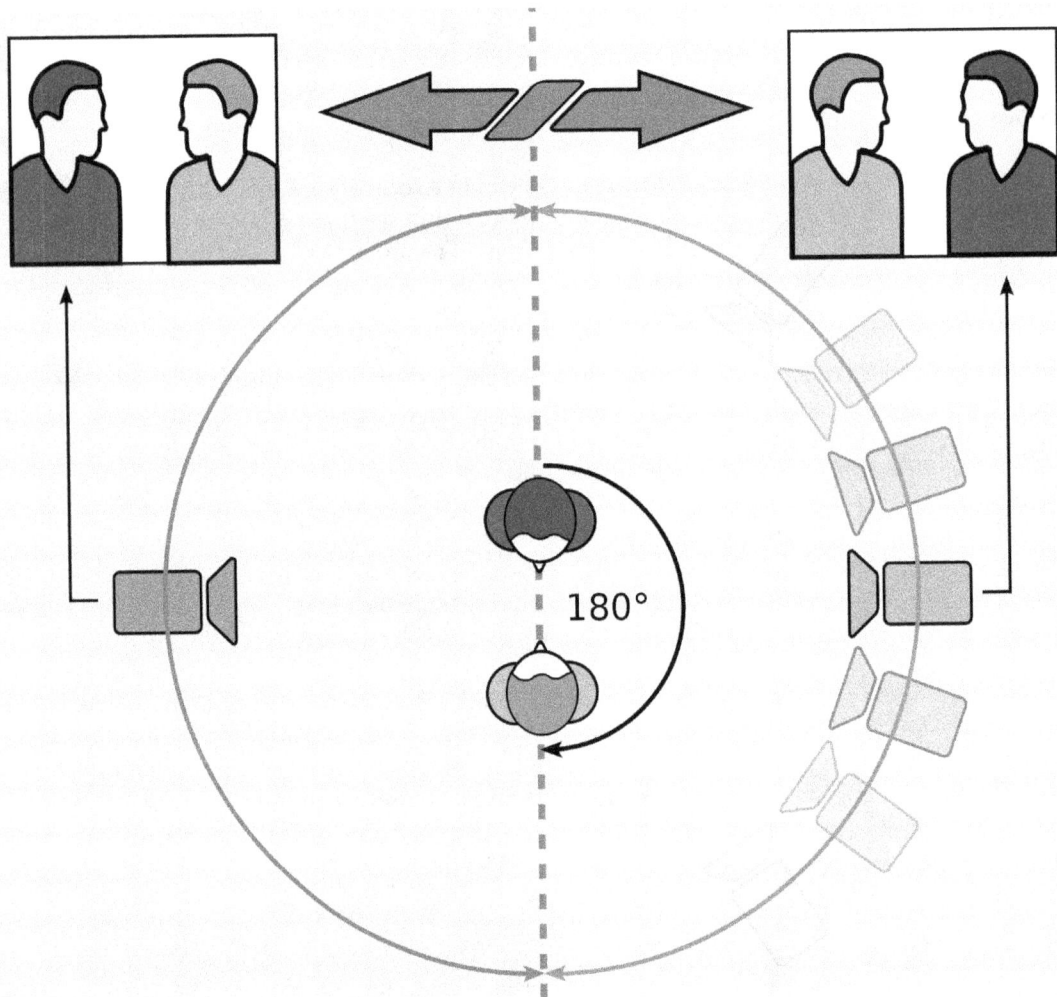

This schematic shows the axis between two characters and the 180° arc upon which the cameras may be positioned (green). When cutting from the green arc to the red arc, the characters' positions switch places on the screen.[43]

and space and another time and space, but depending on the nature of the cut, it will have different meanings.[46]

Cross-cutting is cutting a scene between different sets of action that can be occurring simultaneously or at different times. Cross-cutting is used to build suspense or to show the relationship between the different sets of action.[47]

Fade in[48] and fade out[49] are opposite effects. Fade in is a shot that begins in total darkness and gradually lightens to full brightness. This is a type of transition is similar to "dissolve," which is mentioned below. A sound fade in gradually brings sound from being inaudible to a required volume.

Dissolve is a transition between two shots during which the first image gradually disappears while the second image gradually appears; for a moment, the two images blend in superimposition.[50]

The third type of transition is the wipe. A wipe is a type of film transition where one shot replaces another by travelling from one side of the frame to the other or with a special shape.[51]

A jump cut, which is a term that viewers often hear, is a cut in film editing in which two sequential shots of the same subject are taken from camera positions that vary only slightly. This type of edit gives the effect of jumping forward in time. This is a violation of continuity editing because the continuous time and space are lost as the cut draws attention to the constructed nature of the film.[52]

Editing Example

An example, so you can see how a film is cut and edited or a scene from a film with different cuts shown in it is difficult to find. A YouTube video entitled: *How to Cut a Film – The Secrets of Editing – Film School'd* made by CineFix is good in demonstrating how edits and cuts are done.

https://www.youtube.com/watch?v=ORK8k8_mHyk

Further Viewing

With the completion of this chapter, movies to watch that that are excellent examples of editing are:

- *Sabotage*, 1936, directed by Alfred Hitchcock, starring Sylvia Sidney, Oskar Homolka, and Desmond Tester. This movie is an excellent example in editing by creating the classic suspense scene as to whether a bomb is going to explode at a certain time.
- *Bonnie and Clyde*, 1967, directed by Arthur Penn, starring Warren Beatty, Faye Dunaway, and Gene Hackman. This movie is an excellent example in editing during the bank robberies and the attempts to capture Bonnie and Clyde.
- *The Sting*, 1973, directed by George Roy Hill, starring Paul Newman, Robert Redford, and Robert Shaw. This movie is an excellent example in editing as to what is real and what is not.
- *Jaws*, 1975, directed by Steven Spielberg, starring Roy Scheider, Robert Shaw, and Richard Dreyfuss. This movie is an excellent example in editing by creating a contemporary suspense thriller.
- *Mad Max: Fury Road*, 2015, directed by George Miller, starring Tom Hardy, Charlize Theron, and Nicholas Hoult. This movie is an excellent example in an-award winning best-edited film.

Assignment

Jack has decided to do a shady job—transporting a package of artifacts—with his college friends, Nick and T. J. Jack needs the money to help his close friend, Alec.

When Nick and T. J. enter the room, Nick asks what Jack is doing. Jack tells him. Nick states that the only safe place for the package is on him. Nick states that they can make more money delivering the package than turning it into the police, plus they would not fare too well with the police. Jack states that Alec's life is in jeopardy and the people of the Latin American country should have the treasure returned. Nick asked if Jack is going to be a problem. Nick goes to shoot Jack but T. J. shoots Nick, killing him. T. J. pulls the emergency cord. As the train is stopping, T. J. gives Jack the package and states to give it to the cops. T. J. states he is going to try his luck running, and he disappears.

Alec, Jack's friend, is extremely happy when he wakes up and walks into the living room of an expensive suite for breakfast. Suzie is already in the living room and wishes him good morning and asks him about last night. Alec states that last night was the best night imaginable, and he wishes that it never had ended. Suzie states that last night could only be the beginning and that she took the liberty of ordering breakfast already. Alec states that he is ready for breakfast. Suzie walks over to him, without talking, and kisses him very passionately. As they are kissing, Suzie stabs him three times, lets him fall and states that he now can relive last night forever. Suzie looks at his lifeless body and states that she will love him forever.

The above scenes are the final rising action of the movie leading to the climax. How should these scenes be edited?

37 "Edit," Dictionary.com, http://www.dictionary.com/browse/edit?s=t.

38 "Movie Making Manual."

39 "Footage," Wikipedia, last modified September 7, 2016, https://en.wikipedia.org/wiki/Footage.

40 "Film Studies Program," New Haven: Yale University, last modified September 15, 2016, http://filmstudies.yale.edu.html.

41 "B-roll," Wikipedia, last modified May 4, 2016, https://en.wikipedia.org/wiki/B-roll.

42 "180-Degree Rule," Wikipedia, last modified July 7, 2016, https://en.wikipedia.org/wiki/180-degree_rule.

43 Ibid.

44 "Film Studies Program," New Haven: Yale University, last modified September 15, 2016, http://filmstudies.yale.edu.html.

45 "Montage," Wikipedia, last modified August 17, 2016, https://en.wikipedia.org/wiki/Montage.

46 "Cinematic Techniques," Wikipedia, last modified July 25, 2016, https://en.wikipedia.org/wiki/Cinematic_techniques.

47 "Cross-Cutting," Wikipedia, last modified May 29, 2016, https://en.wikipedia.org/wiki/Cross-cutting.

48 "Fade In," Wikipedia, last modified June 14, 2015, https://en.wikipedia.org/wiki/Fade_in.

49 "Fade Out," Wikipedia, last modified June 14, 2015, https://en.wikipedia.org/wiki/Fade_out.

50 "Dissolve (filmmaking)," Wikipedia, last modified August 12, 2016, https://en.wikipedia.org/wiki/Dissolve_(filmmaking).

51 "Wipe (transition)," Wikipedia, last modified June 6, 2016, https://en.wikipedia.org/wiki/Wipe_(transition).

52 "Jump Cut," Wikipedia, last modified July 20, 2016, https://en.wikipedia.org/wiki/Jump_cut.

8. What Is Sound?

Sound is important in a production. As previously stated in Chapter Four, different aspects of sound enhance the characters and the story, making the movie a complete experience. In addition, we discussed in the previous chapter that sound is edited into the movie so it is coherent and comprehensible within the movie.

But what is sound and how does it enhance a movie?

Sound in a movie includes music, dialogue, sound effects, ambient noise, and/or background noise and soundtracks. Some sort of sound is always used to enhance the movie experience.

Music

Imagine no music in a movie. Certain scenes, like the beginning credits, would have dead air. The movie would seem like it was missing something. Music is a very important element for a movie. In the silent movie period, music was played throughout the whole movie. A film score is the music for a movie. The film score is the music at the beginning of the movie when the credits are rolling, and it sets the atmosphere for the movie.

Have you ever closed your eyes to listen to the music? You can feel like you are being whisked away by the music to a land where the movie is taking place.

Music is also played at critical points during a movie. Have your emotions ever been on edge during a suspense thriller when a certain piece of music is played at different points of a movie? Does your adrenaline start going and your heart start to beat faster during these points of the movie, when you hear that piece of music, because you know something is going to happen? If these situations have occurred to you when watching a movie, how would the movie experience have changed if music was not part of it?

Carefully listen to the music for the first minute and 32 seconds of *Detour*. What kind of comic or serious atmosphere is created for the tone of the movie? What type of atmosphere is created for the protagonist, Al?

Now listen to the beginning music for *Cyrano de Bergerac*. How different the music is compared to *Detour*. What type of atmosphere is created by the music from *Cyrano de Bergerac*?

Dialogue

Dialogue is defined as a conversation between two or more people in a movie. In addition, a movie could have a monologue where a character is speaking out loud when he or she is alone. A character, for example, may contemplate the pros and cons of taking some form of action in a monologue.

A movie can also have voice-over narration. Voice-over narration is when a character is explaining what has transpired in a movie and why. Dialogue, monologue, and voice-over narration progresses the story of the movie.

What would a movie be without dialogue? Even 90 to 100 years ago, there were silent movies with no audio dialogue, but dialogue cards were used, and background music set the tone of the scene. Take a look at the following example of a scene with and without dialogue.

Jack, Suzie and Alec are walking home after work. Jack begins the conversation, as he always does. Suzie speaks, as she is always the first one to respond. Alec is silent for a moment and the other two stop walking. Alec notices that they stopped so he stops walking too. Bewildered, Alec mumbles. Jack retorts. Alec looks at them both. Suzie interjects. Alec returns a comment. After a brief moment of silence where all three look at one another, they shrug their shoulders and begin to walk again.

Suzie questions. Alec comments again. There is silence again and Suzie stops the other two. Suzie speaks. Jack interjects again. Alec calmly states. Jack and Suzie look at each other stunned.

The above scene, with no dialogue but just a description, is only a group of actions with no meaning. They could refer to almost any type of situation. As a viewer, after watching the above scene, would you be interested enough in watching the rest of the movie with no dialogue?

Now read the scene with dialogue.

Jack, Suzie and Alec are walking home after work.

Jack begins a conversation as he always does, "How was the work day?"

"All right," Suzie says as she is always the first one to respond.

Looking at Alec, Jack asks, "How was your day, Alec?"

Alec is silent for a moment as the other two stop walking. Alec notices that they stopped walking so he stops. Bewildered, Alec mumbles, "What?"

"How was your day?" Jack retorts.

"Fine, fine." Alec looks at them both. "How do you think it was?"

"I don't know. That's why I asked."

Suzie interjects, "That's why we asked. We like to know how your day was."

"Oh," Alec returns.

After a brief moment of silence, where all three look at one another, they shrug their shoulders and begin to walk again.

"Wait a minute! You never did tell us how your day was," Suzie questions. "Yeah!" agrees Jack.

"Oh," Alec comments again. There is silence again and Suzie stops the other two.

"Well…" Suzie says. "Yeah," interjects Jack again.

"I quit my job," Alec calmly states. Jack and Suzie look at each other stunned.

The dialogue gives the viewer an understanding of what is going on in the movie. If the above scene was at a beginning of a movie, the viewer would have an idea what the conflict of the movie was going to be.

A contemporary viewer would be lost without dialogue. This is why the version of *The Front Page* has captions. Being released over 80 years ago, in 1931, the sound is not good. So in order not to lose any of the dialogue, the viewer has access to all of the dialogue. Otherwise, the viewer might not comprehend all the dialogue, and the full movie experience could not be obtained.

Sound Effects

Dictionary.com defines sound effect as "any sound, other than music or speech, artificially reproduced to create an effect in a dramatic presentation, as the sound of a storm or a creaking door."[53] An action movie, for instance, is more interesting and bolder with sound effects. With sound effects, the viewer gets more involved with the movie.

Sound effects are most often added into the movie post production. Many times when filming a scene with multiple actions going on at the same time, such as dialogue, sword fighting and other background action, sound effects are added post production to make the effect louder.

In a theatre, watch the beginning scene of *Cyrano de Bergerac*. There are different people speaking at the same time and murmurings of a crowd. Much of this sound would have to be added in later to make it as effective and clear as it is in the movie.

At the 10-minute mark of *Detour*, the sound of the piano that Al is playing is at the same level when the piano was in the background of the scene and when it is in the foreground of the scene. The sound is effective as it draws the viewer to the music and demonstrates Al's ability as a good piano player. Music and sound effects give an aspect of Al's character.

Ambient Noises (Background Noise)

Ambient noises are background noises that are in a room, a house, outside, or any given location.[54] Every location has distinct and subtle sounds created by its environment. Ambient noises are types of sound effects.

As an example to experience what ambient noises are, stand in a room alone and make absolutely no noise at all. The room noises that you hear are ambient noises. A room in an older house would have more ambient noises than a newer home. Also, depending on the neighborhood, you would have outside ambient noises depending on a location. The following are examples of ambient noises: wildlife, wind, rain, running water, thunder, rustling leaves, distant traffic, aircraft engines, machines operating, muffled talking, floors creaking, and air conditioning.

Background noise gives the movie more realism. A movie character is running through a wooded area at night. This scene would lack any suspense if there were no ambient noises.

The sound of the coins in the pouch at the beginning of *Cyrano de Bergerac* is a very important sound because it makes a sound as though there are a lot of coins in the pouch. For this effect, the ambient noise would have to be added in post-production, because that sound would not be able to be heard when filming the scene.

The following YouTube video entitled, "Introduction to Foley and Sound Effects for Film," presented and made by Filmmaker IQ, gives a good demonstration of sound effects and ambient noises.

https://youtu.be/_Jznye0iqYE

Soundtracks

A soundtrack is an audio recording created or used in film production or post-production.[55] Initially, the dialogue, sound effects, and music in a film have their own separate tracks (dialogue track, sound effects track, and music track), and these are mixed together to make what is called the composite track, which is heard in the film.[56]

Late in the 1940s "sound track" became one word, "soundtrack."[57] A soundtrack or an original soundtrack from a movie became a way of advertising the movie.

Further Viewing

With the completion of this chapter, the movies to watch that are excellent examples of sound are:

- *The Haunting*, 1963, directed by Robert Wise, starring Julie Harris, Claire Bloom, and Richard Johnson. This movie is an excellent example in sound, demonstrating what a haunted house sounds like.
- *The Birds*, 1963, directed by Alfred Hitchcock, starring Rod Taylor, Tippi Hedren, and Suzanne Pleshette. This movie is an excellent example of sound as the birds gather and then attack.
- *Silence of the Lambs*, 1991, directed by Jonathan Demme, starring Jodie Foster, Anthony Hopkins and Lawrence A. Bonney. This movie is an excellent example in ambient noises as the protagonist travels to different facilities during her investigation.
- *Hugo*, 2011, directed by Martin Scorsese, starring Asa Butterfield, Chloë Grace Moretz, and Christopher Lee. This movie is an excellent example of sound effects of clocks and different machines.
- *Spotlight*, 2015, directed by Tom McCarthy, starring Mark Ruffalo, Michael Keaton, and Rachel McAdams. This movie is an excellent example of dialogue as an aspect of sound.

Assignment

As Jack, a security guard, is doing his rounds on a college campus, he notices something that he did not see before. He is at the scene of the first robbery, and there was no forced entry. The items were taken, and then the destruction occurred. He goes to the second robbery scene, and he sees the same thing; no sign of forced entry. Jack's mind is spinning as he goes back to the office. He asks Rochelle if she ever goes into the field. She states that she does not because the chief is afraid she will get hurt. Jack then confronts Tom. Jack states that Tom committed the robberies when he was in the field. When Jack discovered the robberies, he noted that Tom was always there to direct the situation and Jack's attention, so Jack would never see there was no forced entry. Tom tells him he is crazy and asks him how he could prove it. Jack says that they are the only ones who have the keys to that area. Jack always assumed there was forced entry because of the destruction. Jack adds that Rochelle never goes out into the field. Tom runs out of the inner office to be stopped cold by Rochelle. When Jack sees that, he tells Rochelle that she is ready to go out into the field.

The next evening the one-act plays are presented, including the one Jack wrote upon returning to college. Jack is on a high because of solving the mystery of the robberies. He believes he may quit college and go back into security and investigations where he belongs. Suzie presents Jack's play. The play performance goes well as Suzie did a good job directing. Jack is looking for her to thank her for a great directing job when Alec, along with two other theatre professors, stop Jack and tell him that the writing of the play was well done. The lines of dialogue are well-written and the action of the play unfolds very logically. Jack is left speechless with a look of astonishment on his face.

What elements of sound, including dialogue, ambient sounds, and sound effects would best enhance these scenes?

53 "Sound Effect," Dictionary.com, http://www.dictionary.com/browse/sound-effect?s=t.

54 "Ambience (sound recording)," Wikipedia, last modified October 29, 2015, https://en.wikipedia.org/wiki/Ambience_(sound_recording).

55 "Soundtrack," Wikipedia, last modified June 13, 2016, https://en.wikipedia.org/wiki/Soundtrack.

56 Ibid.

57 Ibid.

Conclusion: What's So Exciting about Movies? – Novice Answers

We have taken a short excursion to find out what it takes to construct a movie script and then produce it into the final product of a movie. We did not discuss acting and movie stars in this book. Many people will say they get excited about a movie if a particular movie personality is in the movie. But do you? Is that the only reason you go to the movies, or is it a combination of the different elements that we have discussed? If it is only because of a movie star that you go to the movies, you would not have read this textbook. Historically, from a personal novice viewpoint, fans of a particular movie star will stop going to the movies to see this star, if the star has a bad string of movies in a row.

We hope that this brief discussion of movie analysis has proved beneficial. From going through this textbook, you should have a better understanding, so you can absorb everything that you watch, noticing more than ever before in order to get the most out of a movie. So keeping that in mind, what conclusions do you have regarding the construction and production of a movie that can answer the burning question, "What's so exciting about certain movies that continually draw people to them?"

The excitement is a combination of the creativity and originality of the theme, genre, narrative structure, character portrayal, directing, cinematography, editing, and sound. But there is a huge process that has to be done to arrive at the aforementioned right combination of creativity and originality. The whole process is exciting because of what is involved.

The movie begins with a thought or idea by a producer or suggested to a producer by a writer or somebody else. If the producer likes the thought or idea, then the potential movie goes through a five-step process before it is complete and reaches the viewer.

The first step is Development. The Development consists of legally protecting the idea, expanding the idea, writing and re-writing the script based on the idea, creating a budget, and garnering the funds to make the movie.

The Development or Construction step, which was discussed in the first four chapters, is characterized by the following advancements to the movie:

- The theme gives purpose to the movie.
- The genre categorizes the movie but also indirectly shapes the characters and story, establishes the setting, and determines the plot.
- The characters are expanded in order to act within the narrative structure of the story and plot.
- The characters and their actions are further defined by their physiology, psychology, and sociology.

The second step is pre-production. Pre-production consists of preparing a budget for each of the phases; hiring the director and directing staff; hiring the actors and all of the people in the different departments, such as cinematographers, audio mixers, lighting technicians, etc.; preparing the script; and scheduling. The director prepares the script by changing the words into visual shots and scenes.

The third step is production. The production step is the cinematography and audio. This includes the actors, set, lighting, and blocking. The director, as the chief creative person for the movie, oversees this step.

The fourth step is post-production. The post-production stage includes the film score, sound design (including sound effects), and editing.

The fifth step is distribution and marketing. The distribution and marketing are what makes or breaks a movie. How well the movie is marketed determines how many theatre chains and independent theatres will want to show it. The different theatres that want to show the movie will determine how you, as the viewer, will be able to watch, enjoy, and get excited by it.

The preceding is a general example of the process and what happens in each of the steps. It is not all inclusive regarding what truly occurs in each of the steps. The process involves hundreds of people, and it takes several months—possible years—to complete the process.

For this textbook, we concentrated on the middle three steps. These three steps are the exciting heart of the movie and of what most movie viewers are aware. Probably an extreme amount of ideas never make it to the five-step process. Other ideas will only reach a certain step and the whole process will not be complete.

The biggest challenge, though, is knowing the right combination to make a movie successful. This is something that does not have a foolproof plan or formula and will always be a challenge to determine and a chance has to be taken. The right combination of all of these elements makes movies interesting and people will go to see these movies all of the time.

Be a detective and be analytical when watching a movie, or you miss too much, because a lot goes into it, and you can see if it is in the right combination.

Further Viewing

With the completion of this chapter, movies to watch that that are excellent examples of well-produced movies and are the American Film Institute's choices for the best movie of their type:

- *City Lights*, 1931, directed by Charles Chaplin, starring Charles Chaplin, Virginia Cherrill, and Florence Lee. This movie is considered the number one comedy.
- *Snow White and the Seven Dwarfs*, 1937, directed by William Cottrell, sequence director; David Hand, supervising director; Wilfred Jackson, sequence director; Larry Morey, sequence director; and Perce Pearce, sequence director, starring the voices of Adriana Caselotti, Harry Stockwell, and Lucille La Verne. This movie is considered the number one animated feature film.
- *The Searchers*, 1956, directed by John Ford, starring John Wayne, Jeffrey Hunter, and Vera Miles. This movie is considered the number one Western.
- *Vertigo*, 1958, directed by Alfred Hitchcock, starring James Stewart, Kim Novak, and Barbara Bel Geddes. This movie is considered the number one mystery.
- *Raging Bull*, 1962, directed by Martin Scorsese, starring Robert De Niro, Cathy Moriarty, and Joe Pesci. This movie is considered the number one sports film.

Production Assignment

The following synopsis has been optioned by a producer, and he hires you to make a movie out of it. What are the steps you will take to begin the production of this movie?

> The story begins with the introduction of Alec and Suzie, lovers who become engaged and begin to plan their wedding. Everything is going wonderfully until Alec goes to purchase the flowers for the wedding. He enters the florist shop and comes upon a meeting that was supposed to be kept a secret. The members of the secret meeting see Alec and kill him.
>
> This murder so enrages Suzie that she wants to find the people responsible and make them pay for killing Alec and destroying her life, as she knows it. Thus, the second part of the story begins: the conflict or complication, which is finding and dealing with the murderers.
>
> Suzie has a dilemma because she has a notion but has no experience in finding murderers. As a genre, this could go in many different directions. Her complication is huge. With starting at square one, the conflict has to grow logically, with the rising action not being too rapid or slow. The first action is for Suzie to go to the florist to analyze the place to see why someone would be murdered for flowers.
>
> Suzie goes to the flower shop, which is the last place where Alec was seen alive. Suzie looks around the flower shop, but everything looks ordinary, so she cannot figure out the reason for Alec's murder. After 10 minutes of viewing the flowers and flower arrangements, she goes outside and across the street. She stands hidden for hours outside so she can see the rear of the florist shop, but nothing unusual occurs. She does not even see anyone except the one clerk in the florist shop.
>
> She goes home frustrated, wondering why nothing happened, what to do next, and that this does not happen in the movies. In a story, the main character and protagonist has to fail at least once to increase the learning experience of the character.
>
> Suzie is more driven than before to find the reason for Alec's murder. The only thing that she did not do was to go to the florist shop at the same time that Alec did. She returns to the vicinity of the florist shop. She enters the shop because she notices a different clerk and several men shopping in the florist shop. She thinks that this may be nothing, but then she wonders how many men go shopping for flowers later at night. A man may run in and get a dozen of roses, but he would not spend a lot of time in the shop. Coming to this conclusion, she exits the shop before she is stopped by the three men and the male clerk in the store.
>
> She exits the shop and finds a place outside where she cannot be seen but where she can have a fairly good view of the florist shop. In this part of the rising action, a sense of suspense is building, because it appears that something is going to happen.
>
> She sits and watches but cannot hear or comprehend what is going on. She becomes very frustrated. She is also getting angry. She finally storms back to the store and goes in. The men in the store, who appear to have been talking, state that she has to leave because the store is closed. She asks why they are not leaving. They tell her they work there and are in the process of closing. Suzie becomes belligerent and yells that she does not believe them. They go over to escort her out, but she puts up a fight.
>
> She notices a baseball bat and rapidly grabs it. She starts swinging it and hits two out of the three men. The one that was not hit runs away. Suzie continues beating the other two until the were no longer conscious. She throws the bat down and walks out of the store.
>
> Suzie is a changed person because all she can contemplate is maiming the third person that was in the store. She watches the store from across the street night and day for two days but the man

does not show up. Suzie believes that he is afraid of her or what might greet him. Suzie has not found out the condition of the two men she beat into unconsciousness. However, she does not care. She has become callous and hopes that they both die.

Suzie notices that the regular girl who works during the day has come to work. Suzie waits until the girl is at the front counter. She then goes into the store. Suzie states that she is scheduled to talk to an individual that frequents the store. Suzie describes him. The girl states the person is her husband. She apologizes and says that he will not be in the store, because he is still upset with what happened the other night with the other two owners.

Finding out this information, gives Suzie a renewed impetus and energy to get the third and last individual. She knows she is near and cannot stop. Suzie states to the girl that she can go to his house so their conversation does not have to be re-scheduled. The girl states that giving out addresses is against company policy. Rather than arguing the point, Suzie states that it is all right and she leaves.

Suzie leaves the store and waits to right before closing. At that time, Suzie sets up a surveillance of the store again.

Now the climax is getting close as there is only one person left to seek revenge, and Suzie is going to find out where he lives. Suzie follows the girl to her home. Now that she has the address, she is going to return to the home tomorrow with a baseball bat to beat the third murderer of her fiancé.

The next day, Suzie goes to the house. She waits until the girl leaves and makes sure the husband is still at home. Once she sees the husband moving around inside the house, she goes to the front door. She knocks, and the husband comes to the door. As soon as he opens the door, Suzie hits him with the baseball bat causing him to stagger backwards, allowing Suzie to walk into the house, and close and lock the door.

The husband is definitely scared and asks what she wants. Suzie states that she wants to know why the three of them killed her fiancé, Alec. The husband states that it was a misunderstanding because they said that they did not have the type of flowers he wanted so he became belligerent. They tried to restrain him and he accidentally fell, hitting his head. He said that the police agreed that's what happened.

Suzie hits him in the ribs with the baseball bat, breaking some of his ribs and causing him to fall to the ground. He begins to cry that it is the truth and to please believe him because none of them had any reason to kill him. Suzie goes to hit him again as he is lying on the ground, and he sobs as to what does he have to hide? He pleads for her to look at him and his surroundings. Suzie looks at his face and the surroundings. She arrives at a realization and lowers the bat. She states that he is not to say anything. She says that if anybody asks him how he got hurt, that he should just state that he fell. Otherwise, she will come back and really hurt him. He sobs that he will. Suzie leaves.

The next scene is in an office, and Suzie is seen talking to someone, who the audience never sees. Suzie states that she finally realized, at that moment, that she was only seeking revenge out of frustration and that she basically has to start her life over again. She has a difficult time accepting that. The nondescript person states that it will take time. Suzie states that she has never been a violent person. The person swinging that bat never seemed to be her. The nondescript person states that it is time to forgive and begin the long journey back to who she used to be. Suzie agrees.

Cinematography Assignment

The following photos are similar to certain cinematography shots. Answer the questions that are posed in the captions.

What type of shot is this? When and what type of movie would use a shot like this?

What type of shot is this? When would you use this type of shot?

What type of shot is this? When would you use this type of shot?

What type of shot is this? When would you use this type of shot?

Future Viewing

To further enhance your movie viewing experience after completing this textbook, two good sites to go to for a variety of free movies are:

The Open Culture web site, which states it offers, "The Best Free Cultural & Educational Media on the Web": http://www.openculture.com/

Bibliography

"180-Degree Rule," *Wikipedia*, last modified July 7, 2016, https://en.wikipedia.org/wiki/180-degree_rule.

"Ambience (sound recording)," *Wikipedia*, last modified October 29, 2015, https://en.wikipedia.org/wiki/Ambience_(sound_recording).

"Black Comedy," *Dictionary.com*, http://www.dictionary.com/browse/black-comedy?s=t.

"B-Roll," *Wikipedia*, last modified May 4, 2016, https://en.wikipedia.org/wiki/B-roll.

"Character," *Dictionary.com*, http://www.dictionary.com/browse/character?s=t.

"Cinematic Techniques," *Wikipedia*, last modified July 25, 2016, https://en.wikipedia.org/wiki/Cinematic_techniques.

"Cinematography," *Dictionary.com*, http://www.dictionary.com/browse/cinematography?s=t.

"Cross-Cutting," *Wikipedia*, last modified May 29, 2016, https://en.wikipedia.org/wiki/Cross-cutting.

"Dark Humor," *Dictionary.com*, http://www.dictionary.com/browse/dark-humor?s=t.

"Directing," *Dictionary.com*, http://www.dictionary.com/browse/directing?s=t.

"Dissolve (filmmaking)," *Wikipedia*, last modified August 12, 2016, https://en.wikipedia.org/wiki/Dissolve_(filmmaking).

"Edit," *Dictionary.com*, http://www.dictionary.com/browse/edit?s=t.

"Fade In," *Wikipedia*, last modified June 14, 2015, https://en.wikipedia.org/wiki/Fade_in.

"Fade Out," *Wikipedia*, last modified June 14, 2015, https://en.wikipedia.org/wiki/Fade_out.

"Film Studies Program," New Haven: Yale University, last modified September 15, 2016, http://filmstudies.yale.edu.html.

"Footage," *Wikipedia*, lasted modified March 13, 2016, https://en.wikipedia.org/wiki/Footage.

"Jump Cut," *Wikipedia*, last modified July 20, 2016, https://en.wikipedia.org/wiki/Jump_cut.

"Montage (filmmaking)," *Wikipedia*, last modified June 9, 2016, https://en.wikipedia.org/wiki/Montage_(filmmaking).

"Movie Making Manual/Post-production/Editing," *Wikibooks*, last modified July 16, 2012, https://en.wikibooks.org/wiki/Movie_Making_Manual/Post-production/Editing.

"Movies," *Dictionary.com*, http://www.dictionary.com/browse/movies?s=t.

"Romantic Comedy," *Dictionary.com*, http://www.dictionary.com/browse/romantic-comedy?s=t.

"Sound Effect," *Dictionary.com*, http://www.dictionary.com/browse/sound–effect?s=t.

"Soundtrack," *Wikipedia*, last modified June 13, 2016, https://en.wikipedia.org/wiki/Soundtrack.

"The "Basic" Plots in Literature." Special Collections Created by Ipl2. October 13, 2010. Accessed September 16, 2016. http://www.ipl.org/div/farq/plotFARQ.html.

The Voice Foundation, http://voicefoundation.org/about/what–is–tvf/.

"Three-Point Lighting," *Wikipedia*, last modified March 22, 2016, https://en.wikipedia.org/wiki/Three-point_lighting.

Webster's Encyclopedic Unbridged Dictionary of the English Language. Rev. ed. (New York: Gramercy, 1996).

"Wipe (transition)," *Wikipedia*, last modified June 6, 2016, https://en.wikipedia.org/wiki/Wipe_(transition).

Photo Attributions

Still from 'The Front Page (1931), Pubic Domain

Still from "The Driller Killer" (1978), Public Domain

Still from "Cyrano de Bergerac" (1950), Public Domain

"Brooklyn Bridge Park," photo by Guian Bolisay (CC BY 2.0, 2012)

"Day 223-Hang On," photo by Marcus Peaston (CC BY 2.0, 2013)

Wide Angle Shot by Kamil Lehmann via https://unsplash.com/@kamillehmann

Theatre Shot Via: https://stocksnap.io/photo/B1234F8746

Over the Shoulder Angle by Ryan McGuire via: https://www.pexels.com/photo/man-person-school-head-455/

www.ingramcontent.com/pod-product-compliance
Lightning Source LLC
Chambersburg PA
CBHW081258040426
42452CB00014B/2553